T0015802

A

LOOK AT LIFE

FROM THE

FAIRWAY

STEVE CHAPMAN

HARVEST HOUSE PUBLISHERS
EUGENE, OREGON

Bible versions and copyright notifications are located at the back of the book

Cover design by Studio Gearbox

Cover photo © Joseph West Photography / Stocksy

Interior design by KUHN Design Group

For bulk, special sales, or ministry purchases, please call 1-800-547-8979. Email: Customerservice@hhpbooks.com

M This logo is a federally registered trademark of the Hawkins Children's LLC. Harvest House Publishers, Inc., is the exclusive licensee of this trademark.

A Look at Life from the Fairway
Copyright © 2023 by Steve Chapman
Published by Harvest House Publishers
Eugene, Oregon 97408
www.harvesthousepublishers.com

ISBN 978-0-7369-8754-7 (hardcover)
ISBN 978-0-7369-8755-4 (eBook)

Printed in China

22 23 24 25 26 27 28 29 30 31 / RDS / 10 9 8 7 6 5 4 3 2 1

This book is dedicated to
Luther Weathers and Bob Harris
and my fellow golfers
with Golf Outing Fellowship

CONTENTS

INTRODUCTION

I sat down on the passenger seat of our golf cart, and as my friend drove us away from the club-house toward the first tee, he asked, "Why do we like to play this crazy game?" I had an answer I was confident he'd appreciate as he too was a man of faith.

"I think it's a divine design by our amazing Creator. He wired us to be drawn to a particular interest, and He does it for at least two reasons. For our enjoyment because He is a kind and loving Creator, but more importantly, He can use our love of this game as a way to shed light on some life-changing truths that are contained in His written Word."

My answer was based on having had another interest that God used through the years to reveal spiritual insights to me. I discovered in my early teens that engaging in a battle of wits with woods-wise animals like deer and turkey rings the bell of my soul. It's a challenge that has sent me deep into many hallowed hollows to learn how to outsmart wild game, but along the way, as a hunter, I discovered more than food for my body. I found sustenance for my spirit.

These "harvests of truths," as I like to call them, are gleaned when I see something in the outdoors that illustrates a character-building concept in the Word. At other times, I've seen truths in Scripture that were illustrated in the outdoors. It's been a joy beyond measure to experience these links because the yield has been wisdom and guidance I need to help me know my Creator better.

Several years ago, I started compiling into books the helpful and inspiring spiritual insights that have come from my enthusiasm for hunting. The first title was *A Look at Life from a Deer Stand*. Several books followed, and because I was so immersed in writing about the "fair chase," I never considered addressing another topic—that is, until I found that I greatly enjoyed golfing. As I like to say—golf is a lot like hunting because in both you go to the woods and look for something. At least it's true for me.

I suspect anyone who fervently enjoys time on a golf course will agree with that statement. Though it's a formidable challenge to play well, I'm admittedly enamored with chasing and "shooting" that little white sphere around acres and acres of fields and woods. It's a kind of hunting that is just as enjoyable to me as the pursuit of critters—the difference with golf being, of course, I don't have to gut and clean anything when the hunt is over except the bottom of my golf shoes and some clubs.

But just as God used hunting as a classroom where I could learn and better understand His ways, He has used golf to do the same. Of course, in order to enjoy the benefit of the spiritual insights that the game offers, I have to be looking and listening for them, and I gladly and regularly do so with a group of players in Nashville, Tennessee, known as Golf Outing Fellowship (GOF).

With the goal of providing my fellow players with the faith/fairway connections I was seeing, I got the idea to offer bimonthly devotional readings to be sent with the email blasts to the group announcing tee times. Bob Harris, the coordinator of GOF, graciously opened that door, and as a result, this book, *A Look at Life from the Fairway*, was birthed.

If you enjoy the game of golf, my hope is that you will benefit from this collection of quick and easy-to-read entries that feature a key Scripture verse, a short golfing story or scenario that highlights the truth in the passage, and a personalized prayer for your benefit.

Blessings on all your rounds!
Steve Chapman

1

JUST GET CLOSE

As for me, the nearness of God is good for me;
I have made the Lord GOD my refuge,
So that I may tell of all Your works.

PSALM 73:28

M ost of us have stood within short iron distance from the green, and while checking
the pin placement, slope of the putting surface, and
then addressing the ball, we whispered desperately,
"Just get close." Maybe the scorecard to that point
is showing a potential sub-80 round and the longing for that accomplishment is intense, or we're trying just to salvage a round that's gone to the golf
dogs…but for whatever reason, the need to hit it
well and snuggle the ball up near the hole presses
on our nerves.

While these moments in our favored game are

admittedly not critical in terms of life, death, or eternity, they can help us understand just a little better the strong feelings that were coursing through a few notable people who stood at a distance from Jesus and felt a great need to get close to Him.

For example, in Luke 8 there was Jairus, a ruler of the synagogue whose daughter was dying. He felt compelled to get close to the One he believed could heal his little girl. And the woman with the issue of blood who had heard that Jesus could heal her infirmity was surely thinking as she pressed through the crowd toward the Lord, *Just get close!*

Along with these two desperate seekers, Luke 19:3 says of the popular-but-sorely-unliked tax collector named Zacchaeus that he "wanted to see who Jesus was" (NIV). Famously, his small stature and big curiosity drove him into a tree in order to get close enough to see Jesus. His was not a physical life-or-death matter but ultimately a spiritual health concern.

The outcome for all three of these players in the field of biblical history was better than par. Each of them was rewarded with a circle around their story for making their best effort to get close to Jesus. Jairus's daughter was healed, the woman's issue of blood was stopped, and Zacchaeus ended up with Jesus graciously going into his home.

So...the next time that 75-yard approach shot brings up the "just get close" whisper, and no doubt it will, let it be a reminder of the eternal importance of wanting to get close to Christ our Savior. To do so will be the greatest of all accomplishments on or off the course.

◈

Thank You, heavenly Father, for the promise that says, "Draw nigh to God, and he will draw nigh to you" (James 4:8 KJV). I want to get close to You because I know in my heart of hearts that You alone can heal and sustain body, soul, and spirit. In the name of Your Son I ask You to help me to just get close. Amen.

2

THE GREATER
BLESSING

Remembering the words the Lord Jesus himself said:
"It is more blessed to give than to receive."

ACTS 20:35 NIV

A gift every golfer loves to receive during a round comes in the form of "That's a gimme!" This gift of kindness is said in reference to a player's ball that has landed or rolled near enough to the hole that it is deemed unmissable by a fellow player and their putt is not required. With this unearned blessing, the pressure of completing a par, or maybe a birdie or better, or salvaging a hard-earned bogie is immediately lifted off the golfer's shoulders.

While these welcome words are indeed music to the ears when heard, saying them to a fellow player is just as sweet, if not sweeter. For one thing, it's a chance to be on the giving side of Jesus's words: "It is more blessed to give than to receive."

Most of us would agree that as we walk to a fellow player's ball resting near the hole, there's a pure sense of joy that comes with tapping it with our putter across the green in their direction. The thrill of giving in that moment is truly the greater blessing.

Being the giver of a gimme is a wonderful thing for another reason. We get to be an earthly picture of heaven's greatest gimme revealed in the well-known words of John 3:16: "God so loved the world that he gave his one and only Son, that whoever believes in him shall not perish but have eternal life" (NIV).

What a humbling thought that God, our Creator, would love us so much that He would give us the marvelous gift of unearned grace, and with it relieve us of all the worry about whether or not we'll score well in the game of life. This divine gimme is immeasurable in its value and deserves our sincerest gratitude that can be expressed with the same words we say to a friend who blesses us on the green with a gimme. "Thank You!"

◈

Father in heaven, how grateful I am for the gift of saving grace You have given to me. I know I didn't deserve it, yet You saw my need and You met it through Jesus. I want to say thank You by faithfully following You and carrying the light of Your love to others who need to hear about the gift of Your Son that You long to give them. In His name I pray. Amen.

3

WISE WAITING

Even youths shall faint and be weary, and young
men shall fall exhausted; but they who wait for
the LORD shall renew their strength; they shall
mount up with wings like eagles; they shall run
and not be weary; they shall walk and not faint.

ISAIAH 40:30-31 ESV

In a golf instructional video, the teacher showed a
clip of a professional tournament where a player
was standing on the tee box waiting for the group
ahead to move on and clear the fairway. However, a
threesome on the green ahead of them held up the
players who were on the fairway. Consequently, the
wait was longer than usual for everyone.

As the footage showed the scene, the teacher
said, "Take note of what the waiting players are
doing. Each one of them is not just standing

around doing nothing but watching. They have their club of choice out, and they're practicing their swing." He was right. Some of them were doing two-handed rehearsals of their swing, and others were swaying their club back and forth with just their lead arms.

The point that the teacher made with the film clip was how helpful it is to swing while waiting in order to keep the muscles loose and warm as well as remind the brain and body of the swing technique to be used with the particular club chosen for the next shot.

While the players were simply doing what was good for their game, they probably didn't know they were illustrating the profound wisdom contained in today's verse about waiting on the Lord.

In the original language of the Old Testament, the word used for *wait* held the imagery of a vine wrapping itself around a support. In other words, to wait on the Lord means to proactively and intentionally draw close to the One who is our source of strength. Deliberately and daily doing what it takes to be strong in Him is the key to the renewal of the endurance needed to "mount up with wings like eagles" (golfers can appreciate that bird imagery!), to "run and not be weary," to "walk and not faint." But how do we wait wisely?

First, it's important to know that waiting on the Lord to come back is not to be done passively. In the New Testament, the apostle Paul informed the Thessalonians that Christ would return and, on hearing his teaching, there were believers who basically sat down and waited for it to happen. Paul had to help them understand that their passive waiting was an error. To help them be useful to the church by being active waiters, he provided some insight in 1 Thessalonians 5:16-22 on what to do until the Lord returned. His instructions included:

- rejoice always

- pray continually

- give thanks in all circumstances; for this is God's will for you in Christ Jesus

- do not quench the Spirit

- do not treat prophecies with contempt but test them all

- hold on to what is good

- reject every kind of evil

Paul's teaching is as applicable to believers today as it was to the Thessalonians all those centuries ago. Waiting is about biding, remaining, and being present in our relationship with God. With that in mind, the next time there's waiting to be done on a tee box or fairway and some swing rehearsal is happening, let that be a reminder of the "wait training" Paul advised. It's simply wise waiting.

❖

Lord Jesus, I look forward to Your return, but I know it's not wise to just sit down and do nothing while I wait for it to happen. I want to be deliberate with waiting by doing the things needed to stay close to You so that my strength for the journey is renewed daily and so that I can be close enough to hear clearly what You want to whisper to my heart regarding Your will for my life. May it be so in Your holy name. Amen.

4

TAKE ME TO SCHOOL

*The heart of the discerning acquires knowledge,
for the ears of the wise seek it out.*

PROVERBS 18:15 NIV

Every experienced golfer knows the good fortune of their ball ending up in front of and closer to the hole than their playing partner's ball. It might be just inches closer, but the advantage of that position is invaluable in terms of knowledge gathering.

There's a statement that's often said by the player whose ball is inside another's in relation to the cup: "Take me to school." Among friends these words are delivered with a certain level of compassion for the player who is, according to golf etiquette, first to putt. However, if the competition is intense, "Take me to school" might be said, (or wisely just silently thought), with some level of "gotcha."

Whether said with a friendly tone or silently mused in a must-win spirit, the next thing that typically happens is the player to putt second makes their way to a position either directly behind or across the green from the first putter. It's a move that's done for the sole purpose of collecting information by watching the path of the ball as it is sent to the hole. But watching is not all they'll do.

A smart student will also listen for verbal reactions the first putter might give after their attempt, whether it failed or was successful. "Man, they're slow today," or, "Didn't think it was that fast," or, "It didn't move." The insights contained in these post-putt spoken reactions are not ignored by the second putter—if he's discerning, that is.

By using the knowledge gleaned from seeing and hearing, the second putter's percentages for rolling a ball into the cup with just one putt go way up. And it's not wrong to take advantage of the acquired knowledge on a putting green, nor in the rest of life. In fact, according to today's verse, it's a learning process that is biblically recommended *and* commended: "The heart of the discerning acquires knowledge, for the ears of the wise seek it out."

This proverb encourages all of us to be second putters, so to speak. From seeing the legal consequences that someone faced after breaking a law that teaches us not to do the same to hearing a report about someone's success in business that we can apply to our own, the opportunities for acquiring life-enhancing knowledge are endless. And, in my opinion, and maybe yours, there's not a better place to practice this wisdom than during a round of golf.

◈

Father in heaven, I'm grateful for every opportunity I get to glean knowledge that leads to wise living. I ask You to help me recognize those opportunities and to be more discerning when they come so I will hear the instructions I need for making righteous decisions. Because You have gone before me in all facets of living, I willingly and daily ask that You would "take me to school." In Your name I pray. Amen.

5

"JUST WHEN"

*Let him who thinks he stands
take heed lest he fall.*

1 CORINTHIANS 10:12 NKJV

Two words I mutter to myself from time to time on the practice range often bring to mind the apostle Paul's warning to the Corinthians noted in today's verse. Those words are, "Just when!"

To explain, it's when I think I've found a fix in my swing—perhaps a slight tweak in my grip or my takeaway—that results in a half-dozen string of well-hit shots. Then, as excitement swells at the prospect of reaching a new level of consistency, suddenly the next ball flies way left, or way right, or goes dribbling pitifully a few yards in front of where I stand.

Puzzled by not knowing what went horribly

wrong and feeling my ego deflate like a party bal-loon that got in the way of a stick pin, I mumble with disgust, "Just when."

That's my short way of saying, "Just when I thought I had this game all figured out and I am ready to apply for a tour card, get a manager, and hire a caddie, I fall back into a swing-damaging habit."

For a span of a few shots I thought I stood fault-less and my swing would never fail me again. The truth is, I was distracted by a belief that I was better than I am. I didn't "take heed" that I was capable of forgetting the basics and thinking only of the glory that can come with a well-hit driver or iron.

The practice range is not the only place to have a "just when" moment. It can happen off the course too. For example, we can have a few victories over a certain sin—such as an addiction to alcohol, por-nography, or gambling—and begin to proudly think we've conquered the problem. Then, while pompously basking in the distracting glow of suc-cess, we forget that the enemy of our souls still lurks nearby with temptation. Next thing that happens is, the ball of joy is heading into the deep rough.

The question is, how can we avoid the "just

when" moments in our lives? The first step is to understand that, just like in golf, where we are bound to go out of bounds on occasion, so it is true as followers of Christ. We are smart to embrace the "take heed lest you fall" warning and accept the fact that none of us are beyond being tempted.

That admission will then lead to trusting and leaning on the gracious promise that follows in the next verse: "No temptation has overtaken you except such as is common to man; but God is faithful, who will not allow you to be tempted beyond what you are able, but with the temptation will also make the way of escape, that you may be able to bear it" (1 Corinthians 10:13 NKJV).

How good of God to include such an incredibly encouraging and comforting assurance to His followers that He recognizes our weaknesses and is willing to help us get through them. And adding to that good news, just like our bad shots on the course can have an escape route, so it is with temptation. He'll provide a way of escape so that we can get back on the fairway of righteousness.

◈

Heavenly Father, I thank You that You reveal Your strong love for me in my weaknesses. I confess I am prone to proudly think I can stand alone against temptation, but I know it's not true. How good of You to not allow me to be tempted beyond that which I am able to handle. When I am tempted, I will lean on You to help me see the way of escape You provide. Blessed be Your name for such kindness. Amen.

6

IMITATORS

Be imitators of me, just as I also am of Christ.

1 CORINTHIANS 11:1

Paul made quite a bold statement to the Corinthians when he said, "Be imitators of me, just as I also am of Christ." On the surface it sounds brazen and arrogant, but the spirit of his claim was neither. Instead, it was based in humility. Paul knew that if there was anything about him that anyone would ever care to imitate, it was admittedly something he had developed only through being a follower and an imitator of Christ.

What happens among golfers is a good illustration of Paul's assertion. Some of the best golfing advice I've received has been through observation and imitation of pros I'll never know personally but I follow their careers. Stewart Cink is not aware of it, but he is one of my favorite pros. I've gleaned great tips from this ever-fluid, swing-solid, and faith-based man. One August, I intentionally followed him at the TPC in Memphis as he played in the WGC-FedEx St. Jude Invitational tournament. To this day, when I tee up for an iron shot on a par 3, I set the ball at the height I saw Cink use for his shots.

As informative as it is to watch and learn from the pros, most of the valued instruction I've gained has come from players I golf with regularly. When I first began taking the always-exciting-and-often-frustrating journey on the fairways with them, I didn't have much *know how*, but I did have a lot of *want to*. Thankfully, I have been able to imitate some veteran ball strikers in the groups I joined who have helped me turn *want to* into *can do*.

The truth is, the specific skills I have observed in other players I want to emulate are skills they would likely admit were learned from someone else. To be as honest, I would have to do the same. For example, if someone ever watched how I tee a ball up on a par-3 tee box, and they thought it was worthy of trying, I'd have to be honest and say, "Imitate me as I have imitated Stewart Cink."

When it comes to being a Christ-follower, I want to be just as willing, and quick, to repeat the words of the apostle Paul to anyone who might see something in me they want to imitate: "By the grace of God I am what I am" (1 Corinthians 15:10).

◈

Lord Jesus, without Your redemptive love shown to me and Your Holy Spirit, who dwells in me and who teaches me how to live righteously, I would have nothing of value to offer anyone. I want to always be careful to point others to You and Your goodness. May it be so to Your glory and that alone. Amen.

7

GOLD GUY

*It will be like a man going on a journey, who
called his servants and entrusted to them
his property. To one he gave five talents, to
another two, to another one, to each according
to his ability. Then he went away.*

MATTHEW 25:14-15 ESV

My non-golfing wife accompanied me to a local municipal golf course, and at the first tee box she asked, "Why are there four different places for people to tee off, and why are the little markers painted blue, white, gold, and red?"

I explained that someone, at some time, finally figured out that more players would purchase green fees if they felt better about their final score, so they installed multicolored stations for multilevels of driving distance ability off the tee. Of course, I was being a bit facetious about the green fees sales, but the part about the varied tee box setup accommodating the player's ability is a special consideration golfers appreciate.

Because I am a "seasoned" golfer who doesn't have the ability, nor the flexibility, to hit from the max-distance, back-injuring, ego-killing blue box and expect to get anywhere near a gratifying score, I am grateful for the distance break I get as a "gold guy." With that reality freely admitted, I am content to use the spot that allows me to drive according to my ability.

When I approach a tee and walk to the "according to my ability" box, I am sometimes reminded of a similar phrase found in the parable of the talents recorded in Matthew 25. The property owner featured in the story gave three of his servants differing amounts of his talents (a term for money, possibly gold). To one he gave five talents, the second received two, and the third got one. Somehow the master knew the servants well enough that he issued his talents "to each according to his ability." The master counted on his servants to be creative and to be able to show an increase in his talents upon his return.

This parable illustrates that, in the same way golf course designers recognize that players have varying skill levels, God recognizes that each of His servants have different degrees of ability. And just as the property owner expected his servants to use their abilities to multiply his gold, our heavenly Master expects the same from each of us. Whatever ability we have—be it carpentry, managing, or a host of other skills—He wants us to utilize it to advance the precious gold of the good news of His redeeming love for mankind.

In my "gold tee" years of life, I ask myself a question that could also be asked by those who hit from the blue, white, and red boxes: *Am I doing what I can to use my talent in order to give my Master a good return when He returns?*

And return He will.

◈

Dear heavenly Master, thank You for the talent You entrusted me with. I ask for the wisdom regarding how, when, and where to use it so that it won't be wasted. I want to please You and give You a good return on that which You have entrusted to me. So be it in the name of the greatest gift You gave to me— Your Son, Jesus. Amen.

8

SCRAMBLE

*Make my joy complete by being of the same mind,
maintaining the same love, united in spirit, intent
on one purpose. Do nothing from selfishness or
empty conceit, but with humility consider one
another as more important than yourselves; do not
merely look out for your own personal interests, but
also for the interests of others. Have this attitude
in yourselves which was also in Christ Jesus.*

PHILIPPIANS 2:2-5

As far as I'm concerned, a golf scramble competition is just about as fun as it gets on the fairways. While I've heard that "best ball" play can tamper with the quality of a golfer's game by lowering the determination factor, there are simply too many things about it I enjoy to ever refuse the opportunity to participate. Here are a few:

- Playing with friends who also genuinely love the game can be more fun than we should be allowed to have in public.

- Having a single goal as a group and the camaraderie it fosters can build friendships beyond the course.

- The amusing trash talk that goes with a scramble offers the good medicine of laughter.

- Sharing the shot-making responsibilities with other players greatly reduces the pressure to be perfect.

- The "attaboys" that are given with good shots generate good feelings, which in turn can build confidence.

- Grace and forgiveness for unusable, even the ridiculously unusable, shots abound in a scramble—and both are usually evenly distributed among all players over 18 holes.

One other characteristic of a scramble group that's worth noting is how it illustrates the kind of church the apostle Paul was hoping to see in Philippi. He said he'd be filled with joy if the church was:

- *Being of the same mind.* In other words, unified in their belief in Christ. (Like a scramble team needs to think as one player.)

- *Maintaining the same love,* or keeping alive a mutual love for the Lord. (Like the members of a scramble love the game and do what they can to ensure the playing of it.)

- *United in spirit.* (Like each one in a scramble would share a very real inner connection to every aspect of playing golf.)

- *Intent on one purpose.* If each saint would keep a clear focus on their mission as a church, much would be accomplished. (When each member of a scramble team hones in on winning, watch out!)

And here is more advice every scramble team can use. Paul then offers the church some teaching on how to cultivate the unity he desired in their midst. Mainly, his instruction centered on each one making a conscious choice to not see themselves as the center of the church. Instead, if each member would humbly consider others as more important and would look out for their fellow saints' interests more than their own, there was the potential for a powerful, united force for the gospel in the surrounding area. (A scramble foursome, made up of others-centered members like Paul encouraged, would sure be a delight to be on—even if the team didn't win the competition!)

Finally, Paul revealed the greatest of all outcomes that unity and unselfishness can yield. It could be said of those who choose to humbly regard others as more important that they act like Christ. What a tremendous honor that would be! May it be so for all of us both on and off the golf course.

❖

I give thanks to You, Lord Jesus, that although You existed in the form of God, You didn't regard equality with God as something to grasp, but You emptied

Yourself and took on the form of a bondservant and were made in the likeness of men. Yet You humbled Yourself and became obedient to the point of death on a cross (Philippians 2:6-8)...and You did that for someone like me. Help me to have the same attitude in my relationships with family, friends, and fellow churchgoers, as well as those with whom I walk the fairways. In Your loving name I pray. Amen.

9

PAY ATTENTION

*For this reason, we must pay much closer
attention to what we have heard, so
that we do not drift away from it.*

HEBREWS 2:1

I've heard it said that golf is a game of inches and
yards. I can report that the statement is absolutely true because when my driver head is an inch
or so off at impact, I usually end up in someone's
backyard. All seriousness aside, I'd like to blame
my clubs for my unintentional contribution of
pricey balls to course-side residents, but the truth
is, the real problem is a recurring mental condition
I named "lapsafocus."

It would be hard to number the times I've
stepped into a tee box with driver in hand, teed
it up, and without even realizing it, allowed my

47

thoughts to drift away to distractions like the final score, the accolades I would receive when I hit it straight and long, or the envy I would have for the shot my buddy just hit. When that happens, I forget everything I ever heard and learned from You-Tube coaches about setup, ball position, backswing, and follow through. It's not until I look up to see the flight of my shot curling way left or right that I remember that I forgot.

Admittedly, it's easy for my mind to drift, but I know I have to combat this mistake in order to play better. To do so, I've found it helpful to approach every shot with a quiet mental reminder to keep my head in the game. Most of the time I whisper, "Don't think about the total score. Think about the next shot!" If I listen to my own advice and consciously apply the methods I've gleaned from the online coaches, things usually go much better.

When it comes to our walk on the fairway of faith, the writer of Hebrews tells us, "For this reason we must pay much closer attention to what we have heard, so that we do not drift away from it." What does "for this reason" refer to, and what is it that we shouldn't drift away from?

The meaning behind "for this reason" is found in chapter 1 of Hebrews. The gist of the chapter is that the Son of God is immeasurably greater than the angels, and He is "appointed heir of all things, through whom He [God] also made the world. And He is the radiance of His glory and the exact representation of His nature, and upholds all things by the word of His power" (verses 2-3). It's through this Holy One that God has spoken to us, and for that reason we should give Him our constant and undivided attention.

As for what it is that we shouldn't drift away from, the answer is the truths that God has spoken through Christ. When we drift from God's anchor like a boat that's lost its mooring, the end result is that we sink into spiritual defeat.

If nothing else, playing golf can remind us that there are consequences to face when attention is lost, even if for just a few moments. Being defeated by a challenging course or other players because of a drifting mind is not fun, but far worse is losing to sin because of not paying attention to the truths we've heard from Jesus.

◈

Father in heaven, You have my sincere thanks for all You revealed in Your written Word about how to live righteously. I pray for the grace to be ever mindful of those eternal truths and for a greater understanding of them. I don't want to drift in mind or spirit from Your ways. May it be so in the name of the One who is far greater than all the angels of heaven. Amen.

10

GLORY TO GLORY

We all, with unveiled faces, looking as in a
mirror at the glory of the Lord, are being
transformed into the same image from glory
to glory, just as from the Lord, the Spirit.

2 Corinthians 3:18

One of the most enjoyable aspects of golfing regularly with a group of players is watching a newbie gradually improve their game. Week by week, round by round, hole by hole the skill level rises and the stroke count lowers. Along with that, the disappointing moments are fewer and the satisfying moments increase. It's just pure fun and inspiring too!

But really, isn't getting better and better at the game what we all want all the time? Why would we play if mediocrity was the goal? Seeing the scorecard reflect improvement as the rounds go by can motivate us more than anything to keep spending our hard-earned cash on equipment upgrades, buckets of range balls, and the green fees required to test our efforts.

This gratifying feature of golfing is a great illustration of the phrase "from glory to glory" found in today's verse. The implication of the phrase is growth—that is, going from one degree of relationship with God to a higher degree. As He changes us from the inside out through His redemptive work in our hearts, our desire to know Him better and to be more pleasing to Him increases. As a result, His influence in our inner man becomes more apparent, even to us, and thus we experience the thrill of growing from "glory to glory."

Just as a little improvement can go a long way toward bringing us back often to the first tee, growing in the Lord can inspire us to return often to the throne of grace in prayer and to God's written Word for instruction in how our spiritual rounds can progress from glory to glory.

Thank You, Holy Father, for loving me enough to accept me the way I was when I came to You for salvation, and loving me enough to not let me stay that way. Thank You that by Your grace in my life I can not only know You better, but I'll want it to happen. You are indeed a good, good Father. Amen.

11

BALL TALKIN'

Whoever keeps his mouth and his tongue
keeps himself out of trouble.

PROVERBS 21:23 ESV

I t's a curious thing that golfers will talk to their
ball after they have just hit. I do, even though I
know the ball has no ears and can't actually obey my
voice. And even if it did have a way to hear me, do I
really think it would want to listen to the guy who
just creamed it with a blunt object?

Yet for some reason I and most other golfers I
know play under the delusion that yelling at the
ball can change its direction, speed, spin, ground
roll, and destination. Why do we ignore the fact
that all those directives were irrevocably given when
the club head impacted the ball?

Of course, typically the main reason we start

barking orders at a ball in flight is because we think it's heading in the wrong direction, not going far enough, going too far, or any other of the dreaded outcomes we didn't intend. Whatever the case, the only benefit that comes from yelling at a struck ball is that it makes us feel better. Plus, if it was a bad shot, we can blame the cantankerous ball.

Spoken words are like golf balls in flight. Once launched from the blade of the tongue and on their way, they are not coming back. They will land somewhere. Some words have the potential to be helpful, and normally our kind and encouraging words are quietly admired as they fly to their destination. We watch them land and we smile.

What do we do, however, when we know we've hit hurtful words at someone and, after cringing, wish we could redirect them or even call them back? Because we can do neither, there's just one thing we can do. It's what we do when we hit a bad golf shot. We go to the ball and fix the problem. In other words, we do what's necessary to get the ball back on the fairway. In the case of mis-hit words, the answer is an apology. Here's how Matthew puts it: "If you are offering your gift at the altar and there remember that your brother has something against you, leave your gift there before the altar and go. First be reconciled to your brother, and then come and offer your gift" (5:23-24 ESV).

Wouldn't it be great if we never hit another shot from this day forward that was bad enough to make us scream hopelessly at it? Unfortunately, as unlikely as that is, it's also unlikely that we'll never again bean someone in the gallery of our family and friends with some errant words. Though this may be the reality, it should not dissuade us from at least trying to always make the best shot we can with our words. Drawing from Paul's admonition to the Thessalonians, here's what our goal should be with every swing of our "club": "Encourage one another and build one another up, just as you are doing" (1 Thessalonians 5:11 ESV).

Lord, it's no secret to You that I sometimes say things to people I instantly wish I hadn't. I'm grateful You are ready to forgive me when I do, but I want to do better. I pray for the courage to be willing to go to the

one whose heart I may have wounded with my words.
I know that when I do, it not only heals relationships,
but most importantly it pleases You. May it always be
so. Amen.

12

BEEN THERE,
DUFFED THAT

All have sinned and fall short of the glory of God.

ROMANS 3:23

There are at least two good benefits from watching professionals play golf on TV. First, closely observing the many aspects of their skills—such as their setup for tee shots, their hip rotation during their swing, and their greenside chipping skills—is nothing less than a clinic, and except for the cost of the electricity needed to power the television as well as the snacks consumed while on the couch, the instruction is free.

Second, there's a takeaway from tuning in to the tournaments that is encouraging, but in a sort of twisted way. It comes when a celebrated player does something out of the ordinary, like hitting a shot fat that lands short of the green or needing a second attempt to escape from a bunker. While I feel bad for them, I admit it encourages me to know that falling short of perfection happens to the best and worst of us. All I can say to the TV is, "Been there, duffed that."

The fact that all golfers—from professionals to the nowhere-near-a-pro-player like me—are prone to making poor shots is an illustration of a biblical reality about all humans found in Romans 3:23: "All have sinned and fall short of the glory of God." How totally and undeniably true it is.

Of course, making a bad golf shot is not committing a sin, but I find it interesting that the Hebrew word for *sin* is an archery term that means "miss the mark." The difference lies in the mark that's missed. In golf, the hole is the target. In God, being holy (displaying the character of God) is the mark at which to aim. Whether it's in following God or playing golf, falling short is always disappointing but forgivable.

It should be noted that there are a couple of ways to miss the mark both on the golf course and in life. Sometimes a bad strike at the ball is accidental. Maybe it's because a foot slipped on wet, muddy turf during the swing, or a loud, untimely noise caused a shot-destroying flinch. The result is an understandable and acceptable mistake, but it's not deliberate.

As a follower of Christ, it's possible to do something wrong but not on purpose. For example, a person might hear and believe an errant doctrine that sends them off the path of godliness. But then, after realizing the error and returning to sound teaching, the believer can rejoice in having chosen wisely.

Sometimes, however, a "sinful" shot is a product of a deliberate choice. On the golf course, when a player chooses to take a route to the green they know is high on the risk meter, they are deliberately not playing smart. Still, the shot is attempted and maybe a treetop grabs the ball like a tall monster and throws it to the ground, turning a shortcut into a humbling "cut short." The only thing left to do is head to the next shot with plans for a serious course correction.

In a similar way, the person who has willfully and deliberately sinned and then regrets their shortcomings has a need to return to the right path. How does that happen? It's accomplished through repentance. That is, humbly admitting the failure to God and getting back on the fairway of righteousness by trusting the truth that follows Romans 3:23. Verse 24 assures us that we are "being justified as a gift by His grace through the redemption which is in Christ Jesus." Now that's really good news.

It's so easy for golfers to get bogged down mentally and emotionally after deliberately falling short with a shot. But in order to not destroy the rest of the round, they have to move on in hopes for a better experience with the next hole. The same is true for followers of Christ who have become aware of their shortcoming. For the sake of spiritual health and confidence, it's important to trust that God's forgiveness has been applied to the sin and there's no need to wallow in guilt.

What a wonderful thing it is to know there's grace for *all* golfers and especially for *all* God-followers.

◈

Father in heaven, thank You for the grace that covers my failures both unintended and deliberate. Your loving forgiveness is amazing, and I put my trust in it. Blessed be Your name! Amen.

13

THE MADDER YOU GET

Be angry and do not sin;
do not let the sun go down on your anger,
and give no opportunity to the devil.

EPHESIANS 4:26-27 ESV

If the final round of a PGA tournament is on the telly and the scores are close, my beloved non-golfing wife will often join me as I watch it. She likes the drama that builds as the players enlist the best of their skills down the stretch to win the hardware and the cash that goes with it. And she likes to see what the winner's wife is wearing when her hero leaves the green stage.

During a particularly intense Sunday afternoon showing of an event that featured a series of leader changes, one of the players drove his ball into some high rough around the eleventh hole. When he attempted an escape from the salad bowl he was in, the ball dribbled onto the fairway a few feet. His reaction to the less than stellar shot was to furiously bury the blade of his iron up to the hosel into the lovely and lush fairway. That got Annie's full attention.

After bogeying the hole, the same player hit his next drive off course again. We could see the veins in the guy's neck starting to swell with anger even on our small-screen TV. The burn of the sun on his face was made redder by the blood that was boiling in his body. He picked up his tee with a motion that resembled slapping a venomous snake.

As the dejected player walked alone down the fairway toward the ball-search party that had formed, my observant wife said, "Seems to me, the madder you get, the worse you play. He's sure not helping his game by giving in to anger." Then she added. "Anger makes you weak and steals your concentration. It doesn't do anyone any good. I feel sorry for him and for his poor wife too. He needs to get a grip on his emotions."

Everyone watching that irate, club-slamming pro saw a living commentary on the admonition about anger given to us in the book of James. We would be wise to "be quick to listen, slow to speak and slow to become angry." And the answer to why we should follow the wisdom of James is given in the next few words: "because human anger does not produce the righteousness that God desires."

While the uncontrolled anger of the golfer-gone-mad cost him some cash and possibly a better standing in the player rankings, the loss is far worse for those who want to please God yet choose to let rage rule them. Why? Because anger can lead to unrighteous actions, which is the exact opposite behavior that God wants His people to display. That's an outcome we should all strive to avoid.

What, then, is more impressive to God than winning a PGA tournament, or—for the rest of us—posting the lowest score after a round with our friends? Proverbs 16:32 has the answer. "One who is slow to anger is better than the mighty, and one who rules his spirit, than one who captures a city."

◈

Lord, thank You for the challenge Your written Word gives me regarding anger. I admit there are times when I let anger get the best of me, and I know my reaction can be unsightly not just to those around me but to You too. Forgive me for not exercising control, and help me by Your grace and strength to rule over anger. In the name of Jesus, I pray. Amen.

14

WIND—ENEMY
OR FRIEND?

*The wind blows where it wishes, and you
hear the sound of it, but do not know where
it comes from and where it is going; so is
everyone who has been born of the Spirit.*

JOHN 3:8

Every avid golfer knows that one of the main considerations when it comes to shot making is the wind. Because of its effect on the flight of the ball, we want to know how strong it is and which way it's blowing. That's why players and caddies will toss a pinch of grass into the air.

Sometimes the wind is an enemy. If it's a strong headwind, it can knock a ball down like a seven-foot NBA player stuffing the shot of a grade-schooler. For that reason, if the golfer knows how to go low with a drive, they're wise to do so in order to encounter less resistance and achieve more distance. Also, remembering to drop down a club size when fighting the wind is a must.

Sometimes the wind is a friend. Not only is a good tailwind able to give extra-large wings to a ball in flight and add to the carry and total distance, but it can also result in a little more advantage on an approach shot—especially on a par-5 hole. Plus, it can make a golfer walk happily off the tee box with some pep in his step when a shot is pushed farther than usual.

Biblically speaking, the wind has been known to be both an enemy and a friend. As a foe, consider the story in Acts 27 about Paul's experience on the boat that was driven by a fierce wind. The gale was relentless, and eventually the vessel crashed on the rocks. What a powerful enemy the wind was to the sailors and the apostle. Amazingly, all souls aboard survived, thanks to God making sure that Paul stayed alive.

A good example of the wind as a friend is found in Exodus 10, where the plagues are reported that came to Pharaoh for not releasing God's people. One of the plagues was an invasion of locusts.

Pharaoh, in an attempt to be rid of the vast swarm of crop consumers, feigned repentance to Moses and asked him to ask his God to send them away. Verse 19 reports God's response to the prayer of Moses: "The Lord shifted the wind to a very strong west wind, which picked up the locusts and drove them into the Red Sea; not one locust was left in all the territory of Egypt." Even a pagan like Pharaoh could say that the wind can be a friend.

One other scriptural reference to wind that shows it's both an enemy and a friend is especially important to mention. It's found in John 3:8. The verse says, "The wind blows where it wishes and you hear the sound of it, but do not know where it comes from and where it is going; so is everyone who has been born of the Spirit."

In this context, the wind represents the Holy Spirit. He can't be seen but moves in the human heart, giving new and eternal life as He drives away the damaging locusts of sin. The peace that is felt in the redeemed heart is evidence of the moving of the unseen wind of the Holy Spirit. That's how the wind of God's Spirit is, at the same time, a foe of sin and a friend of the sinner.

What a blessed truth to remember on the golf course on a windy day!

◈

Blessed Father in heaven, I will be forever grateful that the wind of the Holy Spirit is a friend of sinners like myself and an enemy of the sin that would destroy me. And I am utterly thankful to be among those of whom You referred to through Your servant John: "Blessed are they that have not seen, and yet have believed" (John 20:29 KJV). I give thanks also for the natural wind that blows and how it can be a clear reminder that You have moved in my heart. Glory be to Your name for such encouraging insight. Amen.

15

THE FIRST
AND THE LAST

So the last will be first, and the first will be last.

Matthew 20:16 niv

On the surface, today's verse sounds like a description of the game of golf because the player who ends the competition last in total strokes is in first place, and the one with the most strokes is in last place. But this verse is obviously not about golf scoring; it's ultimately about God doing what He wants to do when it comes to rewarding people and our choice as to whether to be angry about it or accept it.

Here's the context of the statement. Jesus told a parable of a landowner who hired some vineyard workers. Some he hired early in the morning, some at about nine, some at noon, some at three, and then some around five. When evening came, he paid all of them the same wage. The complaining began when those who started the job early in the morning and worked all day realized that those who started working later received the same wage they did.

The all-day-ers thought they should have been paid more, but the landowner reminded them that they had accepted the terms of employment and—after paying them—he said, "Take your pay and go. I want to give the one who was hired last the same as I gave you. Don't I have the right to do what I want with my own money? Or are you envious because I am generous?" And then the grumblers heard these now well-known words, "So the last will be first, and the first will be last" (Matthew 20:14-16 NIV).

The question this story begs is, would I be upset with God for being generous to someone who didn't work half as hard as I did for the same amount of return? To put it in golf terms, would I be happy if I worked really hard at my game and signed up to play a tournament with a large purse, and then—after battling through 16 holes and gaining a slight lead—I step up to the seventeenth tee and discover the event staff had invited another player to enter the contest at that point? And at the end of the round he would be paid the same winnings as I received? Would I be smiling? I don't think so!

The only possible way I could leave the course with any level of peace in my heart would be to not go home focused on the player who played just three holes and was eligible for a big payday, and also to not be resentful of the tournament staff for their generosity. After all, it was their money to do with what they wanted. The peace I needed would come when I chose to not bellyache about it, but instead be grateful for the earnings in my pocket. In no way would those choices be easy, but they would be right.

As a sidebar to this intriguing parable, perhaps one of the purposes of the story is to help us get ready for what might happen when we get to heaven. There will be those who gave their hearts to Christ early in life, worked all their years for Him, and were rewarded with paradise, and there will be those who accepted Christ on their deathbed who will enjoy the same reward. Whichever end of that spectrum you might be on, remember that God can do with the currency of grace whatever He wants. After all, it's His to give, and we can be thankful that He gives it to both the first and the last.

◈

You are a gracious and giving God who desires to bless everyone with Your mercy and grace. Help me to have a heart of gratitude for that which You have given me and to not be envious of what You want to give to others. In the name of Your Son I pray. Amen.

16

CHOICES

*Choose you this day whom ye will serve; whether
the gods which your fathers served that were
on the other side of the flood, or the gods of the
Amorites, in whose land ye dwell: but as for
me and my house, we will serve the Lord.*

Joshua 24:15 kjv

Whatever total number a player writes down
on their scorecard after 18 holes of golf, he
or she has had to make at least that many decisions
along the way. From where they want to place their
tee shots, to where they would like their approach
shots to land, to how firm to hit each putt needs
to be, making choices is a stroke-by-stroke process
that can be enjoyable—but it can also be energy
draining if the player takes the game seriously.
Here's why.

Every choice a golfer makes is new and unique, and each one has a direct impact on not only the next choice that must be made, but also on the overall outcome. For example, if the player strays off the fairway and decides to risk hitting between two trees to advance the ball instead of chipping safely out on the short grass for a higher-percentage shot to the green, the reward is great if there's success. Not so if timber gets in the way and the ball ends up behind the player. Now another fresh decision is there for the making.

The fact that golf is a constant series of brand-new choices makes it a lot like the rest of life. Each day that comes is a new round filled with decisions. We have to choose whether or not to get up, go to work, attend church, exercise, cook or order in, answer the phone. These and many more decisions are constantly before us.

On a spiritual level, considering how daily, even hourly, that choice making is, could it be that when God inspired Joshua to write on His behalf, "Choose you this day whom ye will serve," He was making it more than a one-time thing? Could it be that with each new day comes an opportunity to reaffirm the choice to serve the Lord? It's certainly true that every new day comes with its temptations and enticements that would lead a believer away from God. Why, then, would it not be necessary to daily reestablish the determination to follow and obey Him?

Each time you gather to play a new round of golf, let it be a reminder that it's more than another day on the course. It's also another day to choose whom you will serve.

❖

Lord, thank You for giving me the choice of whether or not I'll serve You. Because of who You are, and out of thanks for Your great goodness and mercy that You've shown to me and to those I love, I want to declare with each new day, "As for me and my house, we will serve the Lord." Amen.

17

FREEDOM HAS
ITS LIMITS

*You were called to freedom, brothers and sisters;
only do not turn your freedom into an opportunity
for the flesh, but serve one another through love.*

GALATIANS 5:13

The majority of golf most of us play is in the casual category, and it's largely understood and allowable that we can improve a lie before hitting a shot. Many of us do it with a club blade. Some bend down and use their hand to lift the ball out of deeper grass. Others may use the toe of their shoe. Whatever the means, it's a liberty that is generally acceptable among groups of laid-back hackers.

The problem comes when a player uses that liberty as a way to avoid adding ego-killing strokes to the card. Feeling freer about improving a lie than they should, a player might use a foot wedge to move a ball several feet instead of the normal inch or two. That's when the round can turn sour in the soul—that is, if the player cares about writing down a legitimate score in order to finish up fairly.

The golf course is not the only place liberty is abused. In Paul's letter to the people in the Galatian church, he offers a waiver with a warning. The waiver is in his words, "You were called to freedom." It was his way of saying that, because of the completed work of Christ who became their sacrifice for sin, they were not subject to Mosaic ceremonies. The warning followed when he said, "Only do not turn your freedom into an opportunity for the flesh."

Paul urged the people to not use their liberty as a means of guiltlessly satisfying their sensual appetites. The complete, once-and-for-all forgiveness that Christ provided was not to be a license to sin. Instead, Paul wanted them to use their liberty as a way to manifest love to their neighbor and to seek others' edification above their own.

Paul's instruction to the Galatians is just as applicable now as it was then—maybe even more so when you consider the fact that the number of ways that our flesh can be entertained is well beyond what was available in the days of the Galatians.

Rightly taking advantage of our freedom in Christ is a great service to both the individual as well as those they relate to regularly. For example, someone may feel a liberty to drink alcohol, but by not using that liberty to pleasure their palate, they can feel good about not leading a fellow believer into an excess that could harm them. Another person might realize they are free to eat a certain food, but in deference to a neighbor who is weaker in that issue, they choose not to enlist that freedom for the sake of their appetite.

Paul, and the Lord too, would be pleased with Christ-followers who make the kind of choices illustrated in the examples given. Likely, most of us can think of other ways we might be tempted to misuse our freedom. May we be reminded by our occasional and limited use of lie improvement on the golf course to be careful to do the same beyond the eighteenth green.

Father in heaven, I want to please You in every way and every day when it comes to enjoying the liberty I have in You. Help me not make the mistake of thinking Your great grace is my permission to sin. I know that error would hurt me and those around me. Thank You for Your Son who has set me free—free indeed. Amen!

18

THE BLESSED
UNKNOWN

*Do not boast about tomorrow,
for you do not know what a day may bring.*

PROVERBS 27:1 NIV

I f anyone understands that none of us know what
a day might bring, it's a golfer in the tee box on
hole number one. At least it's true for me. I usually
check to see if anyone in my group is standing too
near the tee marker in line with the toe of my driver.
Why? Because I can't be sure that they would not be
the unfortunate victim of a swing disaster.

Often as I'm loading my bag of clubs into my
truck the night before a round of golf, I think, *It'll
be interesting to see what's on my card when I get back
to the house.* Of course, there's no way of knowing

in that moment what only time will tell. And for that reason, even if I'm feeling confident about my game, I'm careful not to boastfully predict what the final tally of strokes will be.

Actually, the unknown is one thing that makes playing golf extra enjoyable and exciting. I said to a friend, "Wouldn't the game be boring if we knew where every shot was going to go?" His answer was, "Yep. It might be boring, but it sure would be lucrative."

Could it be that God, in His great wisdom, made it so that we can't fully and accurately predict what a day holds so that we would learn to trust Him with whatever transpires in all of our days that follow? Not being sure about what a day holds could be called "the blessed unknown" because it's our opportunity to exercise faith. Consider Abraham, for example.

Abraham was a man of great faith, but he didn't know what was really going to happen when he obediently took Isaac up on the mountain to a sacrificial altar. He was willing to go through with the offering of his son, but God provided a replacement sacrifice. What a faith-building outcome Abraham experienced. Undoubtedly, his trust in God grew to a whole new level by the end of that notable day.

We may never face a test like Abraham did, but we daily face the unpredictability of what the next 24 hours hold. It's an awareness that can motivate us to look to heaven for guidance and hope when we wake up. With such uncertainty facing us, it's no wonder that we would want to greet the morning with the singing of, "Leaning, leaning, leaning on the everlasting arms!"

So...the next time you address the ball and prepare to swing away with the troubling feeling of not really being sure exactly where it will end up, and you dare not boast about its final destination, treasure the moment. It's your chance to remember that God alone can be trusted with the outcome of the day.

◈

Lord, thank You that You have all knowledge about what is ahead for me. I want to wake with trust in my heart that You will oversee all that happens to me and those I love. Forgive me for those times that I fail to have faith in Your ability and willingness to watch over my days. Blessed be Your name for caring that much for me. Amen!

YOU JUST NEVER KNOW

The sun's coming up right on time
He fills his cup as he reads the headlines
Gets his keys and heads to the door
But before he leaves he talks to the Lord
He says, "God, it's an uncertain world I'm gonna face
I need You to go with me every step of the way!"

Cause you just never know what a day will bring
No way to know till it's happening
You can plan everything
You can hope you can dream
But till the day comes and goes
You just never know

She gets on the plane, takes her seat
She calls home before it's time to leave
Tells her husband, "I'll be landing at noon
Can't wait to hold you, I'll see you soon."
Then she bows her head as the big engines start
Whispers a prayer and crosses her heart

Cause you just never know what a day will bring
No way to know till it's happening
You can plan everything
You can hope you can dream
But till the day comes and goes
You just never know

Sometimes life will lift up your soul
Sometimes life will lay you low
Not much is certain but one thing is clear
You'll never live in the moment till it gets here[1]

19

LIST OF BENEFITS

Bless the LORD, my soul,
and do not forget any of His benefits.

PSALM 103:2

The game of golf has its benefits, and it's not just cash for the professionals. For example, my wife, who knows I pay to play—as opposed to getting paid for it—notes three benefits that I've gleaned from the game. Graciously she says, "Golfing gives my hubby a reason to get up in the morning, a feeling of accomplishment that comes from improving his skills, and the value of having a circle of friends to share time with."

I am profoundly grateful for my dear wife's listing of these benefits, and I remember them when I head to the course with my fellow unpaid players. It simply makes me feel better and more confident when I'm on the fairways. To forget these benefits would be foolish because I would be forgetting Annie and the benefit of her supportive attitude.

Does this ring a biblical bell for you the way it does for me? Psalm 103:2 calls for us to, "Bless the LORD, my soul, and do not forget any of His benefits." In other words, while you're giving Him thanks for being His child, be sure to remember what comes with that relationship. What are those benefits? The psalmist provided quite a list in verses 3-14. We must never forget that it is the Lord:

> Who pardons all your guilt,
> Who heals all your diseases;
> Who redeems your life from the pit,
> Who crowns you with favor and compassion;
> Who satisfies your years with good things,
> So that your youth is renewed like the eagle.
>
> The LORD performs righteous deeds
> And judgments for all who are oppressed.
> He made known His ways to Moses,
> His deeds to the sons of Israel.
> The LORD is compassionate and gracious,
> Slow to anger and abounding in mercy.

He will not always contend with us,
Nor will He keep His anger forever.
He has not dealt with us according to our sins,
Nor rewarded us according to our guilty deeds.
For as high as the heavens are above the earth,
So great is His mercy toward those who fear Him.
As far as the east is from the west,
So far has He removed our wrongdoings from us.
Just as a father has compassion on his children,
So the LORD has compassion on those who fear Him.
For He Himself knows our form;
He is mindful that we are nothing but dust.

What an incredibly generous God we have. The truth is, David could have written only the first of the benefits on the list, and it would be enough reason to rejoice forevermore. Just knowing and believing that "God so loved the world that He gave His only begotten Son" (John 3:16 NKJV) to provide our pardon from guilt is a blessing beyond measure. But then there's so much more that He gives. If you want to feel better and more confident as you walk the fairways of life, including the long, green, well-manicured type, read the list from time to time, and with a grateful heart remember what's on it.

Father in heaven, there are not enough words to sufficiently thank You for all the benefits You've given me. Your forgiveness alone through the gift of Your Son's completed work of atonement is more than I deserve, yet You generously give infinitely more. For that reason, I can sing, "Bless the LORD, O my soul; and all that is within me, bless [Your] holy name" (Psalm 103:1 NKJV). Amen.

20

PRACTICE 200 PERCENT

*The things you have learned and received and
heard and seen in me, practice these things,
and the God of peace will be with you.*

As a musician and singer, one of the most poignant statements I ever heard in regard to preparing to take the stage was from our son. He said, "If you want 100 percent in your performance, you better practice 200 percent." From then on, when it came to rehearsing, nothing motivated and haunted me more than the echo of those words.

Besides standing before a crowd at a microphone with guitar in hand, there are endless other performance stages in life people stand on, and our son's wise words can apply to all of them. To name a few places where the performer needs to show up prepared, there's the hospital operating room, the teacher's desk, the preacher's pulpit, the jet airliner pilot seat, and yes, the first tee box on a Thursday at a deep-purse golf tournament.

The latter example is of special interest to me and to a host of other outside-the-ropes fans of the game. Though not playing for bread and butter and the pressure that goes with it, serious casual golfers who want to do their best will feel one of the same two feelings pros feel as the tee is pushed into the ground. It's either *confidence* or *consternation*…and it all depends on how ready they, or we, are for the moment of truth.

Golf—what a fantastic way to be reminded of the importance of practice. A day on the course can yield a lot of opportunities (stokes) for a performer to either be glad about the cash spent on range balls or regret that the range was not part of the prep.

When it comes to matters of morality, righteous living, and walking with Christ, in essence we are performers. Our gallery is made up of One, and knowing He is watching would behoove us to practice harder for life off the course than on it.

To help us do that, the apostle Paul wrote, "The

things you have learned and received and heard and seen in me, practice these things." Just prior to that admonishment, he mentioned the following "shots" to work on: "Whatever is true, whatever is honorable, whatever is right, whatever is pure, whatever is lovely, whatever is commendable, if there is any excellence and if anything worthy of praise, think about these things" (Philippians 4:8).

What golfer wouldn't want to shoot true, be honest, pitch right, hit pure, deliver lovely flights, report good scores, and simply strive for praiseworthy excellence? We all do! But the question is, do we want the same in our spiritual lives? I believe we do. And may we keep in mind that if we want a 100 percent result in our performance, we need to practice 200 percent.

◈

O Father in heaven, I give thanks that in You and through Your written Word I can learn, receive, hear, and see how to live so that I can journey in confidence through this life. I want to practice to please You, Lord. You alone are good. Amen.

21

READING THE BREAK

"My thoughts are not your thoughts, nor are your
ways My ways," says the LORD.
For as the heavens are higher than the earth, so are
My ways higher than your ways,
and My thoughts than your thoughts."

ISAIAH 55:8-9 NKJV

The fact that upward of 50 percent of a successful golfer's practice is on the putting green is proof that the easiest physical stroke in golf is the hardest to do consistently well. Typically, you're using the shortest club in the bag. It has a flat-faced blade that doesn't have to be forced through turf, and unlike a driver or iron swing, nearly 100 percent of the time the takeaway and the swing spans a few inches or, at most, a foot or two. So why, then, is the easiest stroke the hardest?

Besides the fact that the hole is relatively small compared to the entire green and seems to get smaller the closer the putt, the answer to why putting can bring sweat to the player's brow and cause shaky hands is in a list of considerations that must be addressed prior to execution (a word that is fitting for many putts):

- green firmness
- surface obstacles
- grass height
- grain direction
- roll speed
- wind speed
- green slope
- the break (or breaks)

Perhaps of all the considerations named, green slope and breakage may be the most elusive to pin down for most golfers, including the pros. Accurately reading the undulations in order to avoid the frustrations of a miss is a quest that seems to show up about 18 times per normal round, and, of course, sometimes more than that when we come up short or roll one too long.

As haunting as it is for golfers that the word *break* is part of the word *heartbreak*, there is at least one redeemable thing about the putting challenge. It's an illustration of an eternal truth that is humbling, to say the very least. To explain, if the green with its hard-to-figure contour could speak, it could say what God said of Himself: "My thoughts are not your thoughts, nor are your ways My ways." That reality is proven true over and over with misreads that can leave players groaning with disappointment.

The obvious takeaway with this comparison is that in order to be successful with a putt, the green's ways must be studied, understood, and submitted to. Thus, the walks around the cup, the plumb bobbing, and the squatting (if knees allow) to determine slope, along with any other reads that can be made before the putt.

In the same way that we must take the time and effort to study a green and accept its variations, it's necessary to closely consider the ways of God so that our thoughts are changed to His regarding how to rightly navigate the hard-to-predict breaks in life. If we fail—or worse, refuse—to do so, the only result will be the groan of spiritual heartbreak.

❖

Father in heaven, I give You thanks for the heads-up that Your ways are not mine. I admit my need to know Your ways and Your thoughts, and I thank You that You have provided a divine "Greenbook" in the form of Your written Word that shows me all I need to know about You. Though I am prone to misread situations and have done so too often, I want to do better. Thank You for Your grace to help me do just that. In Your name I pray. Amen.

22

SCARS OF LOVE

He Himself bore our sins in His body up on the cross,
so that we might die to sin and live for righteousness;
by His wounds you were healed.

1 PETER 2:24

To get ready to play in a scramble that our church was sponsoring, I went to my front yard with my 5-iron to see if that wonderful swing was still not there. After several swipes at unsuspecting clumps of grass, our then-eight-year-old daughter, Heidi, stepped out on the front porch and said, "Hey, Dad, can I try that?" I said, "Sure," and invited her to join me.

I handed Heidi my adult-sized iron and said, "Give it a go." Though the club was weighty in her young hands, she took a stance and then a full swing. I was impressed. She had a natural form, and a word came to my mind when I saw it. *Scholarships!*

"Heidi," I said with some excitement, "your swing flows nicely. Come here and I'll show you something helpful about swinging a golf club."

I had her back up to me, and while behind her I put my hand on her head, tilted it downward, pointed to a small white clover bloom, and said, "Now swing the blade of the club back and forth over that clover and see if you can make it pass over it each time while keeping your head still." What happened next is still a bit of a blur.

When she heard the word *swing*, she did just that, only it was a full swing. Hearing me gasp at the sudden realization I was in harm's way, she tried to stop the heavy club, but it whipped in her hands, causing the toe of the blade to careen into my left cheek just a little south of my eye.

I reeled off into the yard in pain and instantly put three fingers of my left hand over the impact site. I could feel a knot rising under my fingers as I staggered backwards. I stopped and took my fingers off the hump on my cheek, and I was shocked to see blood squirt like a water fountain out of my face. Heidi saw it too and screamed as she ran into the house.

I thought my beloved daughter had left me out there to die, but she ran to get her mother. Annie came out, saw the crimson carnage, and hurried back in to get a towel. Within a few minutes, I was on my way to the ER, where I got a total of eight stitches.

While I was at the ER, my mother (who was visiting) took Heidi to a nearby store to get a card for me. When I got home, she gave it to me and didn't say a word as she studied the bandages on my cheek. The card had a frog on the cover sitting on a lily pad. Heidi had drawn a scar on its face, and on the inside the message read, "I feel like pond scum." It was an apology card.

I sat down and invited her to sit on my lap. In that moment, I gently hugged my little girl and said two things to her. "Heidi, please know that I love you and I'm not upset. The good part of all this is that now I can say I spent time with my kids and I have the scars to prove it." She smiled and relaxed. Then, seizing the opportunity to turn the trauma into a teaching moment, I added, "And there's someone else who loves you very, very much and has the scars to prove it. His name is Jesus."

◈

Lord Jesus, from the depths of my heart I say thank You for the proof of Your love, which is shown in the scars on Your precious hands that reach out to save a sinner like me and Your feet that willingly walk beside me to guide me through this life. Blessed be Your name for such compassion. Amen.

23

SWING LIKE A GIRL

Charm is deceptive, and beauty does not last;
but a woman who fears
the LORD will be greatly praised.
Reward her for all she has done.
Let her deeds publicly declare her praise.

PROVERBS 31:30-31 NLT

I won't forget the day I was finishing up a round
of golf with some friends, and in sight of our last
green was the final fairway of another of the three
nine-hole courses we were playing. I noticed all
the players were young females. It was a parade of
ponytails streaming from the back of baseball caps.

Realizing the players were competing in a tournament between two colleges, I took a moment and
watched a couple of the ladies hit their approach
shots onto the adjacent green. The golfing skills I

observed made my jaw drop. I was amazed at how effortlessly they seemed to strike the ball...and how far they hit it with incredible accuracy.

Stunned at seeing such fluidity and power in their swings, I thought to myself, *From now on, if anyone ever says to me, "You swing like a girl," I will smile and respond with a proud and grateful, "Thank you."*

As the girls putted out and headed to the next tee, I wished I could have followed them to watch and learn, but there was a round to complete. Later that day, when I remembered the sight of such skill on display, I realized there are many ladies who can teach a man a thing or two, and not just about golf. A host of women can show mankind some important and life-changing lessons about character and strength. Some of them are in the Bible. To name a few...

- Jochebed, mother of Moses, influenced history by surrendering the child she loved to the will of God.

- Miriam, the sister of Moses, played an important role in the exodus of the Jews from Egypt.

- Deborah was an influential female judge. Because of her wisdom, faith, and leadership, Israel knew peace for 40 years.

- Ruth was a virtuous young widow and an ancestor of King David, whose descendant was Jesus Christ.

- Hannah, the mother of Samuel, was an example of perseverance in prayer. Barren for many years, she prayed unceasingly for a child until God granted her request. Then she gave the boy back to God.

- Esther saved the Jewish people from destruction, protecting the line of the future Savior, Jesus Christ.

- Mary, the mother of Jesus, was a touching example of total surrender to the will of God. When an angel told her that she would become the mother of the Savior through the Holy Spirit, she endured the potential shame and birthed the Son of God.

These women in the Word are not the only females that men, whether golfers or non-golfers, can look to for improving our game of life. From caring mothers to loyal sisters to faithful teachers, their virtue can be a clinic on how to live rightly. And if a man is fortunate enough to have a mother, a sister, a wife, an aunt, or a female friend who fits the description of the woman featured in Proverbs 31, he is blessed beyond measure and would do well to thank God often for her.

❖

Thank You, Father, for the ladies in my life who exemplify good character and enduring strength. How wonderful it is that You have seen to it that women like this are noted in Your Holy Word. I want to be careful to learn from each one what You want to teach me. Amen.

24

WHAT I WANT
TO DO, BUT DON'T

I do not do the good I want to do,
but the evil I do not want to
do—this I keep on doing.

ROMANS 7:19 NIV

My third shot onto a long par-5 green required some shaping if I expected to get on the putting surface that was about 150 yards away. Between my ball and the green was a short line of three, 30-foot-tall trees. Bending the shot around them with a draw would do the trick.

I addressed the ball with a seven-wood, closed my stance and the clubface a little, took a couple of practice swings, moved in, and prepared to enter the moment of truth. No one wanted the shot to work more than me, but no one was more disappointed than I was when, instead of going around the trees, my ball flew directly into the first one and made that distinct and disturbing crackly sound as it impacted the branches.

As I watched the ball drop straight down to the ground not 30 yards away, I had to face a fact that had a biblical ring to it. What I did was not what I wanted to do, and that which I didn't want to do, I did.

If you've read Paul's letter to the Romans, you can see why his words are an accurate assessment of my attempted shot. The interesting thing about Paul's candid admission that he struggled with doing life righteously is that there's encouragement in it.

To think that Paul, the great apostle and author of a good portion of the New Testament, admitted that his intentions and his actions didn't always work out is something I can certainly relate to as a follower of Christ, and likely you relate to it as well. But if we read more of what Paul said, we find hope.

> If I do what I do not want to do, it is no longer I who do it, but it is sin living in me that does it. So I find this law at work: Although

I want to do good, evil is right there with me. For in my inner being I delight in God's law; but I see another law at work in me, waging war against the law of my mind and making me a prisoner of the law of sin at work within me. What a wretched man I am! Who will rescue me from this body that is subject to death? (Romans 7:20-24 NIV).

And now comes Paul's comforting answer to our great dilemma of wanting to do good but not doing it:

Thanks be to God, who delivers me through Jesus Christ our Lord! So then, I myself in my mind am a slave to God's law, but in my sinful nature a slave to the law of sin. Therefore, there is now no condemnation for those who are in Christ Jesus, because through Christ Jesus the law of the Spirit who gives life has set you free from the law of sin and death (7:25–8:2 NIV).

I admit that these thoughts from Paul are not easy to understand. But what I do glean from them by reading carefully is that I can rest in the truth that if I'm in Christ Jesus, though I fail to consistently do good, God knows the intent of my heart, and He does not condemn me for it. What He notices is my "want to." Desiring to do things right, even though I don't always do it, finds His favor— and pleasing Him is, and must always be, what I want to do.

O gracious heavenly Father, I give You my deepest thanks for recognizing that the greatest longing in my heart as Your child is that my life would be pleasing to You. Because of Your Son, Jesus, who set me free from condemnation when He carried my failures to the cross, I can live worry-free and at peace with You. Blessed be Your name for this great and everlasting hope. Amen.

25

THE SPOTTER

*My eyes are on all their ways; they are
not hidden from My face, nor is their
wrongdoing concealed from My eyes.*

JEREMIAH 16:17

It's good to have a friend spot for me as I hit a drive. I appreciate the courtesy, but I must admit it can be both helpful and haunting. It's helpful to have an extra pair of eyes to watch where my ball goes. It's haunting because there's an extra set of eyes watching where my ball goes—and watching me swing. The outcome can be either awesome or awkward, depending on where the shot lands.

To be so completely exposed to the observing eyes of a fellow player is a bit unsettling, but it can also be comforting to know that if my shot is wayward, there is at least some hope that the ball will be found. These contrasting feelings are not unlike those that Jeremiah 16:17 can bring to the heart of anyone who is aware that "the eyes of the LORD are everywhere, keeping watch on the wicked and the good" (Proverbs 15:3 NIV).

The words from Jeremiah were given as a warning to those living in God's land who were defiling it through disobedience to His commands. While the warning was stern, the end goal was the eventual restoration of a people who were to occupy the land and worship God in holiness. Like a spotter on the tee box is there for our good, so it is for our good that we have God's presence in our lives as our Watchman.

HE'S WATCHING

Whatever you're doing behind that door
Don't forget the eyes of the Lord are watching
He can see you.

You can pull those shades way down low
And think nobody sees what you really are,
but He knows
He can see you.

Nothing is hidden, nothing gets by
Nothing is hidden from the all-seeing eyes
Of the Lord, He's watching.

You can wait until the sun goes down
And in the cover of the nighttime
You can sneak around
But He's watching, He can see you.

But if you lift those shades
If you open that door
If you walk in the light
You won't have to worry anymore
That He's watching, He can see you.[2]

◈

Thank You, my compassionate and loving heavenly Father, for being my heavenly Spotter. Knowing that Your eyes are always on me and that I cannot hide my ways from Your presence is a blessing beyond measure because I know You have my good in mind. Help me to daily live before You in a way that is obedient so that You can find pleasure in my time here on earth. In the name of Jesus, I ask this. Amen.

26

THE SUN DOESN'T RISE

*God exalted him to the highest place and gave
him the name that is above every name, that
at the name of Jesus every knee should bow, in
heaven and on earth and under the earth, and
every tongue acknowledge that Jesus Christ
is Lord, to the glory of God the Father.*

PHILIPPIANS 2: 9-11 NIV

The Korn Ferry Tour came to the Nashville, Tennessee, area in the spring and, while checking to see the tee times for the players, I was surprised to discover that the first pair of threesomes off the number one and ten tees was scheduled for 6:35 in the morning.

I assumed the early groups would likely arrive at the course at least an hour before dawn to warm up. That meant they would be there about the time the big orange ball would make its appearance on the eastern horizon. At least they had that awesome event to take away the sting from such an early start.

Being a golfer, I have yet to tee off as early as those Korn Ferry boys. However, I've seen many sunrises through the years. My encounters with the slowly growing and glorious light have been in the hunter's woods. And it was during one of those magnificent morning cosmic shows that something dawned on me that was life changing. Here's how I described it in a book for hunters titled *A Look at Life From a Deer Stand*:

> The event we have always called "sunrise" is actually a divine illusion. What happens is far more spectacular than we may have realized. Instead of rising, the sun remains stationary. It doesn't revolve around the planet. Instead, it is the earth that makes the move. As it spins on its axis, the earth bows to the sun. What a beautiful picture of the only solution for a human heart that suffers from a void of heavenly light. It must humble itself in the sight of a never-changing God. And at that moment, His light rises up, warms the heart, and blesses all who see it.

God longs to be revealed in every heart, including yours. If you have not allowed Him that divine action, please remember that Jesus said, "I am the light of the world; he who follows Me shall not walk in darkness, but shall have the light of life" (John 8:12). Today is the day of salvation! Let Him into your heart. Then He will gladly say of you, "You are the light of the world" (Matthew 5:14). May the Lord give you courage to allow Him to be the Sonrise in your heart.[3]

O God our great Creator, You have made an incredible world for me to live in, and it's filled with amazing testimonies of the work of Your mighty hands. The event that I call sunrise is one of the most awe-inspiring of them all, and it's amazing how it can remind me daily to bow my knee before You so that the hope-giving light of Your grace will rise in my life to guide me and bless those around me. I don't want to hide Your glory by allowing pride to rise up in my heart. For that reason, I humbly pray for Your

help to always be mindful to acknowledge that You alone are God. In the name of Jesus, may it be so. Amen.

27

THE GAME IS IN THERE!

*Blessed be the God and Father of our Lord Jesus
Christ, who has blessed us with every spiritual
blessing in the heavenly places in Christ.*

Ephesians 1:3

H ere's the unfolding scene…
It's my second shot. I'm standing behind
the ball on the fairway surveying the green that is,
according to my rangefinder, 135 yards away. I pick
out a spot where I want my shot to land, and then
I step forward and shift sideways left of the ball. As
I recheck the lie, I take a couple of practice swings
with my trusty iron and then move in to take my
stance.

I first make sure the blade of my club is facing the target correctly, double-check the landing
spot, settle in, feel my lead arm straighten with

my elbow toward my belt, and slightly tighten my three-knuckle grip. Then, as I take the club back, I remember to time the bend of my left knee and the rotation of my hips, push off with my right leg, and keep my hands ahead of the ball through the downswing. All the while I stay positive and coax myself to expect a crisp hit.

After completing my practiced technique of letting my right shoulder bring my head around at the end of the follow-through, I look up to find the ball in flight. Suddenly, a flood of excitement, as well as gratitude and relief, rushes in when I see it flying exactly where I aimed. I lower the club and watch the ball hit the green 20 yards in front of the hole, bounce once and a half, then roll toward the cup, stopping about two feet from the pin. There's a noticeable pep in my step now as I walk toward a possible birdie putt.

In those all-too-rare occasions when I hit a good, BYB ("bring ya back") shot, I usually whisper to myself and sometimes to those I'm playing with, "Well…the game is in there!" What I mean is, not many of my shots turn out as well, but when it does happen I can say with confidence that everything

I would need to learn to repeat that kind of hit—such as my muscles, joints, hand/eye coordination, instinctive distance calculation, and so on—were in me when I was born.

On a spiritual level, a BYB shot on a golf course is a commentary on the truth in Ephesians 1:3 that says, "God…has blessed us with every spiritual blessing in the heavenly places in Christ." In other words, when a person is born again, the Father in heaven places in them everything needed to "learn the game" and grow from a child to a man in terms of spiritual maturity. For example, God gives the blessing of His grace and strength to believe and obey His commandments, the blessing of a desire and determination to please Him, and the blessing of assurance that whatever happens in life, He can be trusted with the outcome.

To put it another way, every grown male golfer at one time was a smooth-faced infant. In our little bodies is every element needed to grow a beard. It just took time for it to happen.

So maybe the next time you hit that BYBer, stop for a moment, bask in the shot glow, and let it remind you that by His grace "the game is in there!"

❖

Father in heaven, I give thanks to You that I have been blessed with every spiritual blessing in the heavenly places in Christ, Your Son. All I'll ever need to walk worthy of being Your child was given to me at my rebirth. I pray for Your help to grow daily in You and put those blessings to good use so that I may be pleasing to You. In the name of Christ I pray. Amen.

28

"QUIET, PLEASE!"

Be still, and know that I am God!
I will be honored by every nation.
I will be honored throughout the world.

PSALM 46:10 NLT

The quip "silence is golden" is especially applicable during a round of golf. While some international competitions (such as the men's Ryder Cup or the Solheim Cup for the ladies) welcome and encourage unrestrained, boisterous cheering from each side's gallery even during shot making, at all other events, including the local casual play, being quiet during someone's swing and putt is expected etiquette.

Those who would ask what's so important about moments of silence on the course have likely never mis-hit a critical shot because they flinched at the sudden sound of someone talking mid-swing. They don't understand how fragile the mind can be when it's immersed in concentration about their take-away and follow-through technique and the outcome they're trying to achieve.

We've all heard the inconsiderate types who seem to always be outside the ropes at professional tournaments as gallery members. Being silence challenged, it takes everything in them to be quiet at the appropriate times. These are the onlookers who hold it in until just before the club head impacts the ball and then explode with an ear-piercing, "Get in the hole!" Either they want to go home and watch the recording to hear themselves yell, or alcohol has tampered with their better senses, or both. But, as annoying as their outbursts can be, at least they partially understand that silence has its place in the game.

It's also noticeable at pro tournaments that stillness is not just a vocal issue. It includes not being a visual distraction. Standing still and being quiet go hand in hand. Thus the reason for volunteer monitors around each tee box, fairway, and green who stand with "Quiet Please" placards raised while a shot is attempted.

Simply put, stillness during someone's golf stroke is more than a tradition; it's a matter of respect and honor to the player. And because experienced golfers appreciate the gift of silence—not only received but also given—the purpose of the psalmist's words, "Be still, and know that I am God!" is not lost on us.

We understand that being quiet before the Lord means being able to listen to His voice. And like gallery members who want to learn something from the highly skilled player that will help them get better at the game, being still before God is an opportunity to watch and learn from Him how to be better at life. For that reason, it's always a welcome request from the divine course monitor, the Holy Spirit, when He says, "Quiet, please."

◈

Lord, how well You know that it's not always easy for me to show You the honor You deserve by being still before You. I want to not only be quiet so I can hear You speak to my heart, but I also want to stop moving so I can see You move in my life. Thank You for allowing me an activity like golf, where I can practice both how and why to be still and know that You are God. Amen.

29

THE CART PATH SPEAKS

*Jesus answered, "I am the way
and the truth and the life.
No one comes to the Father except through me."*

JOHN 14:6 NIV

It would be interesting to know how many total miles of cart paths exist on golf courses across the world. No doubt the number would be staggering. These well-used trails made of concrete or asphalt are placed along fairways with thoughtful consideration given to how the appearance of the property is affected, as well as how players will continuously move from tees to greens.

We don't think much about cart paths during normal playing conditions except when our driver or long iron puts a ball in flight that touches down on the hard surface. How many of us have said, as the ball clicks loudly on impact, "Give me some of that cart path, baby!" We say it because we know that our 200-yard drive will turn into a 240 yarder. The ball might be scarred a little, but the added distance is always welcome.

The cart path also gets our attention when we play after a heavy rain. That's when we hear those expected-but-dreaded words from the staff behind the desk when we go into the clubhouse to cover our green fee: "It's cart path only today." When that announcement is made, we're well aware that any ball that doesn't land somewhere near the cart path is going to require more walking than we might prefer to do. But because we care about the course conditions, and we prefer to not be escorted from the premises, we comply.

It was on one of those ground-drenched, cart-path-only days at an unfamiliar course that I saw something about the cart path that had a biblical ring to it. As I sat in our rented cart waiting for my buddy to walk across the fairway to hit his second shot, I looked at the long ribbon of man-made rock ahead of me and thought, *We don't know our way around this course, but if the path below me could speak, it would say, "I am the way."*

Those are the exact words of Jesus. He told His disciples, "You know the way to the place where I am going" (John 14:4 NIV). Thomas said to Him, "Lord, we don't know where you are going, so how can we know the way?" (verse 5). That's when Jesus replied, "*I am the way* and the truth and the life. No one comes to the Father except through me" (verse 6).

Carefully notice that Jesus didn't say "I am *a* way." He intentionally and boldly said, "*the* way." This truth about Him is confirmed in 1 Timothy 2:5-6 that says, "There is one God, and there is one mediator between God and men, the man Christ Jesus, who gave himself as a ransom for all" (ESV).

Some folks consider it narrowly dogmatic to say that Jesus is THE way to the Father. Yet it's the message they need to hear. Besides, there's nothing wrong at all with the narrowness of the claim. To illustrate that it's wise and caring to give a definitive answer about who Jesus is, consider this situation. If a golfer is at a course he doesn't know well and asks someone where an unseen flag is on an elevated green, he wouldn't benefit by an answer like, "Just hit it up there anywhere you think it would make you happy." There's no help at all in that reply. The benefit comes when the question is answered with something like, "See the tops of those three pines beyond the crest of the hill? Aim for the middle one, use your 90-yard club, and you'll do well."

Because the golfer's score is on the line, the quality of the advice regarding the whereabouts of the flag is found in its specificity. Far more important than that is the truth that our eternal lives are on the line when it comes to finding our way to the Father. For that reason, being dogmatic and narrow on the topic of salvation is a must.

With that in mind, the unloving thing to say to someone who is searching for true salvation is that there are many ways to find it. On the other hand, the loving thing to say is, "This is the testimony: that God has given us eternal life, and this life is in His Son. He who has the Son has life; he who does not have the Son of God does not have life" (1 John 5:11-12 NKJV).

Now perhaps you'll never see a cart path again without remembering those life-changing, hope-yielding, love-giving words, "I am the way."

❖

Blessed Father in heaven, I give You my deepest thanks for providing Your Son, Jesus, as the way to You. I believe it with all my heart, and I ask You to help me be bold, caring, and loving enough to let others know this eternal truth. In the name of Jesus, may it be so. Amen.

30

GRANDBIRDIES

Grandchildren are the crown of the aged.

PROVERBS 17:6 ESV

On any given morning in any season of the year, when the weather is tolerable or even near tolerable, foursomes by the droves are made up of seniors lining up at golf courses all across the country to play another round together.

I am glad and thankful to say that I am among the masses of gray-haired, gold-tee golfers that I refer to. In the group of guys I have joined, many have the extra time to head to the course a couple of days each week because they're retired. These fine gentlemen gather for fun, fellowship, and to see if that marvelous swing is still there...or not there. And there's the conversation to enjoy too.

One of the subjects I especially enjoy hearing

and talking about in my group of seasoned players is grandkids. With the reports of what hilarious
things the grands have said, we can provide plenty
of proof that Art Linkletter was absolutely correct
when he said, "Kids say the darndest things."

We all agree that one of our most important
responsibilities in our later years involves our
grandchildren. The influence we can have on their
outlook on life and their future is not something
to be taken lightly. This is especially true when it
comes to helping them maintain good morals and
a godly character.

Perhaps one of the most powerful commen-
taries on this fact is found in John 8:9. The verse
comes near the end of the well-known story about
the woman who was caught in the act of adul-
tery. The men who were judging her had stones in
their hands and were preparing to put her to death.
That's when Jesus stepped in and challenged them
with the well-known response, that was essentially:
"Those without sin cast the first stone" (John 8:7).

Their response should be noted by every grandfather and grandmother.

"They which heard it, being convicted by their

own conscience, went out one by one, *beginning at the eldest*, even unto the last: and Jesus was left alone, and the woman standing in the midst" (John 8:9 KJV, emphasis added).

Note carefully the words "*beginning at the eldest*." The probing question that this detail raises is, if the eldest in the group had chosen to not respond to the convicting words of Jesus, but stayed instead to follow through with the killing of the woman, would the youngest have done the same? Likely, and what a tragedy it would have been for the older and the younger as well.

Another question this story raises applies to grandfathers today. Is there anything that we are doing that we sense in our hearts is wrong and that we should walk away from in order to lead our grandkids to righteous choices? May God help us be good examples of holiness to our grandbirdies so that we can be worthy to wear "the crown of the aged."

◈

Father in heaven, I offer my sincere thanks for letting me live long enough to see my grandchildren. I want to be a good influence on each one, to lead them away from sin by my own turning from it. Forgive me for where I may have failed my grandkids, and help me from this day forward to keep the welfare of their future in mind as I make choices today. In the name of Your Son, Jesus, I pray. Amen!

31

FAITH AND
THE TEE BOX

Faith is the substance of things hoped for,
the evidence of things not seen.

HEBREWS 11:1 KJV

It's always a curious thing to watch a pro golf tournament on TV and see the tee area lined on both sides with gallery members. Sometimes the dual lines extend 30 to 40 yards toward the hole from the tee box markers.

With the camera showing a view from behind the player teeing off, the sight of fans excitedly leaning in to watch the action makes me cringe a little when the big "what if" is considered. What if the pro has a momentary lapse of skill and line drives one face-high into the gallery right or left? It hurts just to imagine the results.

A mis-hit by a highly skilled pro is not inconceivable, yet the onlookers ignore that fact and put their complete trust in the pro, believing they are perfectly safe in his or her hands—hands that are gripping a long shaft tipped with an oversize mallet that, when swung, travels somewhere between 110 to 130 miles per hour and, after impact with a rock-hard ball sends it screaming in their direction at around 140 or more miles per hour.

If it didn't take that much speed for David's rock to kill Goliath, there's no way a golf fan would survive being pummeled in the face by a stray dimpled stone. Still, the masses clamor for a place right by the ropes. What are they thinking? I don't know what's on their mind other than wanting to witness greatness, but I do know what they have to exercise when they're staring into the pro's lightning-fast driver face.

It's faith!

Whether they know it or not, it takes enormous faith for each onlooker to believe they will not suffer a deadly blow from an errant tee shot. Perhaps their trust is in the reputation of the pro's consistency in the tee box, or maybe they're simply mentally numbed by the excitement of the moment.

With its inherent risks, the tee box experience for trusting fans seems to be a good illustration of the biblical meaning of faith. First of all, faith is "the substance"—or the assurance—"of things hoped for." Of course, what the fans feel sure about is that they won't get beaned by a badly hit ball. It's as though they believe they were given a title deed to that outcome when they bought a ticket to the tournament that features only the highly skilled in the game.

The "evidence of things not seen" is a sense of confidence in the mind that when the ball leaves the club face, they'll hear it whoosh by, and—with a snap of their still-intact head toward the ball in flight—they'll breathtakingly watch it travel around 300 yards and land somewhere in the distance.

Where does that confidence come from? History! They have likely seen that particular player hit his or her drive straight down the fairway time and time again without incident, and their reputation for not inadvertently killing a bystander has earned their trust—but not all of mine.

I don't have that level of faith in mankind no matter how well developed their swing is. There's always the possibility of a toe-hit disaster, and I don't want to be the one in the news who didn't live to tell about it. For that reason, if I'm ever in a tee box gallery, I'll be behind the player (a wise thing to also do while playing with friends, no matter if their handicap is 1).

Ultimately, there's only one "driver" who merits my utmost faith. His name is Jesus. Those of us who believe in Him can agree that His reputation of never, ever failing is all the evidence we need in our hearts to trust that He can and will do that which is otherwise undoable. What a blessed hope to have as we walk on the fairway of life!

◈

Heavenly Father, what a wonderful gift faith is. The privilege of trusting in Your unfailing love—and the hope that it brings to my heart that I will someday see fully with my eyes what I can now only believe in my heart—is a reason for rejoicing. And it's a reason to keep following You. By Your grace, I want to do just that for all of my days. Amen.

32

MARKERS

Samuel took a stone and set it up between
Mizpah and Shen, and called its name Ebenezer,
saying, "Thus far the LORD has helped us."

1 SAMUEL 7:12 NKJV

Placed in the ground on the eighteenth fairway of East Course at Merion Golf Club in Pennsylvania is a square bronze plaque that says:

June 10, 1950
U.S. Open
Fourth Round
Ben Hogan
1-Iron

The history of that shot is that Hogan had ground his way through to the seventy-second hole and needed a par to have a chance to win. With a stiff wind in his face, he took a 1-iron from his bag, a club that was notoriously hard to control. Amazingly, Hogan's ball flew onto the eighteenth green, resulting in a two-putt par that got him into a playoff that he would win the next day against George Fazio and Lloyd Mangrum.

Any golfer from then on who plays by that well-deserved plaque gets a reminder of the golfing miracle that took place on that summer day. The rare marker is there not just to commemorate greatness, but also to inspire it.

While it's true that most of us who regularly play golf will never have a metal marker to recognize a great shot, we do have mental markers at spots on courses that are personally notable. Each time we go back and play in that unforgettable place, the remembrance of what happened there inspires confidence and a determination to repeat the moment.

Whether it's for Hogan's unbelievable shot or one that we personally consider incredible, what makes each of them rise to the level of deserving either a metal or mental marker is usually that the shot is made in the face of adversity. Hogan had survived a car crash that nearly killed him. Yet he fought through and rebounded to the point that he was able to play again. It was with a body that had suffered an array of injuries that Mr. Hogan pured his 1-iron onto the green from the fairway.

For you or me, perhaps the shot that merited a mental marker was not made through as great a challenge as Hogan's. Still, it's considered worthy of remembering. Maybe it was out of the thick rough or one from off the fairway that needed to sail between the forks of a tree, or maybe a shot from a deep bunker without the pin in sight that rolled up next to, or into, the hole.

In the same way that the Hogan metal marker and our own mental marker represents a victory in the face of adversity, so does the stone that Samuel set up between Mizpah and Shen.

The people of Israel had gathered at Mizpah, and the Philistines heard about it and approached them to engage in a battle. However, "the LORD thundered with a loud thunder upon the Philistines that day, and so confused them that they were overcome before Israel." Then, "the men of Israel went out of Mizpah and pursued the Philistines, and drove them back" (1 Samuel 7:10-11 NKJV).

It's no surprise that Samuel would want to erect

a memorial to that victory. Of course, Samuel knew well that the outcome was God's doing, and with the stone he wanted to help the people remember that important detail. How many of us, beyond the golf course, can look at places in our lives where we know God helped us overcome a situation?

Maybe it was a family crisis, a health crisis, financial battle, or some other intense challenge that we fought to win, and we know without a doubt that God saw us through to the victory. And now that time and place is duly marked in our hearts, and when we need renewed courage to press on we can return to it, like we do with those great shots we've had, and say what Samuel said, "Thus far the LORD has helped us."

Father in heaven, I am grateful that in times of trial and challenge I can pray with the psalmist who said, "I will remember the deeds of the LORD; yes, I will remember your wonders of old. I will ponder all your work, and meditate on your mighty deeds" (Psalm 77:11-12 ESV). Amen.

33

THE SEARCH

I love those who love me;
and those who diligently seek me will find me.

PROVERBS 8:17

When our son returned from a two-day stay at the Masters in Augusta, Georgia, he brought some tournament swag for me that included a glove, a couple of nice green hats, and box holding a dozen golf balls distinctly marked with the Masters logo. I debated about actually taking any of the items to the course with me, but I couldn't resist the temptation.

There was something uniquely satisfying about opening a sleeve of three brand-new bright and clean Masters balls and letting one roll out into the new glove on my left hand. Instantly, I felt a bond to it and held it with hopes that we would be together for the next 18 holes and well beyond. However, my hopes were dashed when I teed off on the third hole and sent the dimpled treasure off the fairway into some high grass under some huge oak trees. Thankfully, after an intense and nervous search, I found the ball. Today's featured verse is about searching and finding something of great value. It says, "And those who diligently seek me will find me."

While this statement could apply to man's search for God, it's not what the promise refers to. It's about wisdom, which is poetically personified as a female in Proverbs 8:1-3: "Does not wisdom call out? Does not understanding raise *her* voice? At the highest point along the way, where the paths meet, she takes *her* stand; beside the gate leading into the city, at the entrance, *she* cries aloud" (NIV, emphasis added).

What claim does wisdom make that we should love her and seek for her? Verses 6-8 reveal just some of her value: "Listen, for I have trustworthy things to say; I open my lips to speak what is right. My mouth speaks what is true, for my lips detest wickedness. All the words of my mouth are just; none of them is crooked or perverse" (NIV).

And verses 10-11 raise wisdom's stock in a big-time way. "Choose my instruction instead of silver, knowledge rather than choice gold, for wisdom is more precious than rubies, and nothing you desire can compare with her" (NIV).

Perhaps the next time you have to enter into seek mode on the golf course, you'll not only be reminded that nothing you desire—including that brand-new golf ball you hope to find, and the low score you want to get with it—can compare to the value of finding the riches of the wisdom that are hidden in Christ. And the good news is, though you might not always find your precious and pricey ball, it's guaranteed that you'll always find wisdom if you love her enough to go look for her. If that happens, you can rejoice because…you win!

◈

Father in heaven, I want to love wisdom enough to seek You diligently and daily and to understand who and what You are. I ask You to open my eyes as I search for You in Your Word, and that through it You'll teach me Your everlasting ways of holiness and righteousness so that, in finding, I will be found pleasing to You. In the name of Christ, the One who has all wisdom and knowledge to give, I pray. Amen.

34

DON'T MOCK THE GAME

Do not be deceived: God is not mocked...For the one who sows to his own flesh will from the flesh reap corruption, but the one who sows to the Spirit will from the Spirit reap eternal life.

GALATIANS 6:7-8 ESV

Most of us, during one round or another, have yielded to some type of self-deception and have paid the price for it. For example, after a tee shot on a par 4 that didn't find the fairway, you might be standing beside your ball that's resting near a very tall tree that stands between you and the green. While the smart thing to do is to use your 5-iron and punch it under the branches back onto the short grass, you listen instead to the voice of unreason that says: *Don't be a pansy. You have the lie, you have the power, and the top of that tree is no match for your 52-degree wedge. Show those guys how it's done. Go for it!*

Then, as you do the swing-finishing pose that pros do, your heart sinks at the all-too-familiar sound of a clump of leaves catching the ball like an outfielder stealing a home run. As the ball falls to the ground a few yards away, you face the regretful cost of an extra stroke and promptly, and humbly, put your 52 away and pull your 5 out of your bag.

Basically, what just happened is that you mocked the game of golf by deceiving yourself and ignoring your skill limitations. This pricey mistake is a worthy illustration of the disaster that can happen when God is mocked.

God is mocked when a person pretends to know, love, and serve Him but really doesn't. Claiming to be His follower yet willfully ignoring His laws and choosing ways other than those that please Him is described as sowing seeds of sin that will yield fleshly corruption. As my wife put it when she heard about a bank robber who ended up in jail, "If you break God's laws, God's laws will break you."

The good news is that there's a flip side to this picture. Going back to the wayward shot near the tree, accepting your limitations and choosing to punch it back onto the fairway is sowing the seed of wisdom. The crop that it can yield is a doable approach shot and a much better chance for a par. Far better than a par save is "the one who sows to the Spirit (the Holy Spirit) will from the Spirit reap eternal life."

What does it mean to "sow to the Spirit?" The best answer to that question is found in Psalm 1:1-3: "Blessed is the one who does not walk in step with the wicked or stand in the way that sinners take or sit in the company of mockers, but whose delight is in the law of the LORD, and who meditates on his law day and night. That person is like a tree planted by streams of water, which yields its fruit in season and whose leaf does not wither—whatever they do prospers" (NIV).

The bottom line is, don't mock the game of golf, and by all means, don't mock God. Very simply, both are smart play!

◈

Father in heaven, I don't want to be guilty of mocking You by claiming I am Yours and yet not obeying Your commands. Forgive me for those times I've been guilty of thinking that my attitude and actions are not seen by You, and for intentionally ignoring the right choices and going my way instead. I want to plant my life in the Holy Spirit so I can reap the harvest of eternal life with You. May it be so in Your name and to Your glory. Amen.

35

BLISS OR THE BUCKET

A cheerful heart is good medicine, but a
crushed spirit dries up the bones.

PROVERBS 17:22 NIV

If ever there was proof that a "cheerful heart is good medicine, but a crushed spirit dries up the bones," it would be in the game of golf. Any experienced player knows that every round can have as many, and likely more, low and high points as there are holes to play. This being obvious, is there more to the words of Proverbs 17:22 than meets the eye? The answer is yes.

Note how close together the contrasting statements are in the verse. Only a little comma separates the swing from cheerful to tearful. It takes hardly any time to go from one to the other. Actually, it can happen as fast as it takes to turn the smile on your face to a frown. Try it now…that was quick, wasn't it?

The swift transition from "fun-ishment" to "pun-ishment" is not lost on golfers. We know that one shot can make us feel happy and uplifted by the stress-relieving medicine that the joy provides, and with the next shot the soul can feel squashed like a bug under a boot.

The same is true, of course, in the rest of life. In one moment we can experience the optimism-building, scientifically confirmed, immunity-boosting benefits that come with laughter, and the next minute something can happen that devastates the emotions and can even stiffen our joints—like a phone call in the middle of a peaceful night's sleep from the police department, or a letter in the mail-box that comes in the middle of a beautiful, sunny day—from the IRS!

The question is, how do we handle the inevitable, emotional shift from happy to sad? If you were to ask my wife, she would tell you what she told our four-year-old granddaughter a few years ago when she suddenly went from giggly to groaning over not getting her way while playing with her cousins. As the tears dropped like rain from our grandchild's cheeks, Annie said, "Young lady, you have a choice. You can either choose to be happy or you can choose the bucket."

The "bucket" is a reference to what our grand-daughter usually did when she became terribly upset. She would get in such a bad way that she would get sick and hurl. Thus, the need for a bucket.

Our little GrandChap frowned as she thought about it for nearly a minute and finally said, "I'll choose to be happy." At that point, the choice of a cheerful heart was the medicine she needed to heal her wounded spirit. She wiped the tears away and went on about her playtime with her cousins.

From that day on Annie has said, "If a four-year-old child can understand the value of choosing to be cheerful, then I can do it too. I'll take bliss over a bucket any day!"

We think our granddaughter was able to choose cheer because she was somehow able to understand that her only other choice was the pain of sadness. And the sadness would only separate her from the fun her cousins were having.

In life, and on the golf course too, each of us has

a choice when it comes to dealing with the onset of sadness. There may be good reason for it, but eventually, if we want to enjoy cheer and freedom from the pain of dried bones, or the joy-stealing disappointment of a bad golf shot, we would be wise to choose to "be of good cheer" (John 16:33). It's either that—or the bucket.

Lord, You know very well how hard it is for me to choose to be cheerful. But as challenging as it is, that's how much I want to apply the healing balm of a cheerful heart to my spirit. And, though it's not easy to say that it's a good thing for me, I thank You for the opportunities to learn to turn to cheerfulness instead of sadness. Let Your joy overflow in me, even into my dry bones! In Your name I pray. Amen.

36

YOUR OWN SWING

Therefore, my beloved, as you have always obeyed,
not as in my presence only, but now much more
in my absence, work out your own salvation with
fear and trembling; for it is God who works in
you both to will and to do for His good pleasure.

PHILIPPIANS 2:12-13 NKJV

The golf swing has one purpose, and that is to impact the ball with a chosen club in order to move it ahead as accurately as possible toward the next hole. While there is a widely used traditional type of swing that incorporates the familiar and very dependable motions like that of Ben Hogan, not all swings are as uniform—not at all.

Some notable players in the past who had an unconventional swing are the late, great Arnold Palmer with his side-bending, head-tilting follow through. And there's the incomparable, powerful flick of the Raymond Floyd swing. More recently the names Jim Furyk, and the highly unusual Matthew Wolf can be mentioned. Both are known to sort of whirlybird their clubs before impact, and Wolf adds an extra "say what!" when he appears to curtsy to the fairway just before his takeaway.

Besides these examples, many of us likely have observed someone in our circle of friends who has a quirky movement somewhere in their swing, yet as their ball flies straight and true we realize that the difference may be distinct but obviously works for them.

Often, whenever I see a player with a swing that is uniquely theirs, I tend to assume that at some point in their lives they realized that inside them was a strong desire to play golf. With the motivation of believing that the game was in them, they may have set out on their own to bring it out and put it on display. As they did, they found a motion that had good and consistent results and stuck with it. It's a process that is promoted in the Bible.

In Philippians 2:12, Paul urged the saints at Philippi to "work out your own salvation." Note that he didn't say work *for* your own salvation, but work it *out*. There's quite a difference. He was saying that Christ was in them already since they had believed in Him and accepted the free gift of salvation that God offers. On that basis of truth, he wanted each one to work out their salvation by letting God's presence in them be displayed. By working *out* their salvation, they would display the light of God's grace to a dark and dying world around them, thus advancing the gospel.

As a golfer, very likely at some point in time you realized that inside you was the game of golf. You didn't have to work *for* it to be there, you simply worked it *out*—you found your own swing, and now you outwardly show others what is uniquely within you. Spiritually, as a believer who openly displays God's presence that is in you by daily living in obedience to Him, you are advancing the good news of redemption through Christ.

As you work out your own spiritual swing, so to speak, keep in mind two important and encouraging facts. One, you can rest in knowing that, as Paul said, "It is God who works in you both to will and to do for *His* good pleasure" (verse 13). Two, you can expect to look different to the world as it observes your "swing" because, as Peter points out in 1 Peter 2:9, you will be among those who are "a peculiar people; that ye should shew forth the praises of him who hath called you out of darkness into his marvelous light" (KJV). So…go forth, swing away, and let Christ shine in you. The world needs to see Him through your unique story!

◈

Father in heaven, I am grateful that You would work in me the eternal gift of salvation through Your Son, Jesus. I want to do Your will and bring to You the good pleasure of my obedience. Help me to be a living witness of Your grace and to serve You and others in the unique way that You have designed for me. May it be so to Your glory and that alone. Amen.

37

FRIENDS

A friend loves at all times, and a
brother is born for adversity.

PROVERBS 17:17 ESV

There's an observation about friendships that I can say from experience is absolutely correct: "With friends, joys are doubled and sorrows are halved." This truth can be seen clearly among friends on the golf course. There'll be joyful high fives when a birdie is made, high tens with an eagle, and high tens plus a chest bump or two with a hole in one. The joy does indeed double in those times. But then, there's the other side of the saying.

When sorrow comes with a tee shot that bounces into a lake or maybe a missed two-footer for a desperately needed par, there's consolation in a friend's understanding words like, "They shouldn't have put that lake there…hit another one," or, "Great putt. You got robbed."

Mess-ups like these in the context of casual golf are not major tragedies; still the sharing of the sorrow is sweet. But there are other sorrows during a round that can be an unexpected call to rally around a friend. I remember, for example, getting to the eighth hole of an 18-hole round. The weather was perfect and everyone was shooting well. Then one of the players' cell phone chirped. He wisely answered because it was his wife calling. His face went ashen as he said, "I'm on my way."

His wife had suddenly taken ill and an ambulance had been dispatched. We stopped the game and said a quick prayer for his wife as his cart mate sped him off to the parking lot. Calls of concern for the situation were made as the day progressed, and later the husband reported that his wife was doing well and expressed how much he appreciated his buddies sharing the anxious hours that followed the unexpected call on the eighth hole.

As the husband was whisked off to his vehicle that day and the rest of the group took him and his beloved to God in prayer, the words of Proverbs

17:17 that say, "A brother is born for adversity" were put into action. Our friend, who seemed a bit paralyzed by the news about his wife, was in need of our faith, sort of like the paralytic whose story is recorded in Mark 2:1-12.

In the account, Jesus was teaching in a crowded building, and the paralytic's friends, in a desperate move to present him to Jesus to be healed, ripped off the roof of the room and lowered their needy friend down to the noted Healer. Mark records this reaction: "When Jesus saw their faith, he said to the paralyzed man, 'Son, your sins are forgiven'" (verse 5 NIV). And along with that forgiveness, the man was healed, took up his bed, and walked home.

It's important to note that the verse says that it was his friends' faith, not the paralytic's, that got the attention of Jesus. What a great story to motivate each of us to be ready and willing to be there in times of trouble that a friend might face, whether it's a simple bad golf shot or the upsetting, round-ending news that comes by phone.

What a wonderful gift You have given us, Lord, through the love of friends. I have been blessed by both the joys I've shared with friends, and the comfort I've received from their words and actions in hard times. For that reason, I want to do the same for my friends by recognizing and responding to their joys and sorrows. I want to do it just like You would, for You have been, and will always be, the best friend anyone could have. Amen.

38

THERE'S ALWAYS HOPE

The hope of the righteous brings joy.

PROVERBS 10:28 ESV

Before I left the parking lot of the local course where I had just finished 18 holes with some friends, I called my wife to let her know I was coming home. When she answered, the conversation went like this:

Annie: "Hello."

Me: "Hey, babe. We're done and I'm heading your way."

Annie: "How'd you do today?"

Me with my best subtle explanation of the outcome: "I had a great round going, then we teed off on number one."

167

Annie, with compassion: "Well, maybe dinner will heal your wounds."

My dear bride knew I was dealing with disappointment. She could hear it in my voice, and I was grateful for her understanding words. To further console me, she added, "There's always hope that the next round will go better for you." It was not only the perfect thing to hear, but it was also absolutely true. It took just five miles of my thirty-mile drive back home to recover from a lousy score and to start looking forward to some fairway redemption.

When it comes to golf, hope is a constant companion. It might wane for a minute or so after slinking away from an on-in-two with a three-putt hole, but usually during the walk to the next tee the thought, *I'll do better this time,* brings a certain amount of expectancy that lifts the spirit.

This roller-coaster ride with despair and hope doesn't just happen from a green to the next tee box, it happens with every challenging shot. I'm continuously thinking hopeful thoughts like:

- *I believe I can hit to the green out of those trees.*

- *Surely, I won't blade this chip.*
- *This bunker shot is going to be spectacular.*
- *Ain't no way I can miss this three-foot putt for par.*

The fact is, it's the constant return of hope for a satisfying game that keeps me smiling through an entire round, even if it is a bust. And the gladness that comes with that hope is always enough to make me want to try again. But as sweet as it is, there's something even more special about having hole-to-hole hope. It's a great reminder of the heavenly hope that I need here on earth. It's where joy is found in the journey of faith.

Today's verse from Proverbs says it clearly. "The hope of the righteous brings joy." The question is, who is the righteous, and what joy is being highlighted? The righteous person is, of course, someone who has put their faith and trust in the Son of God, dwells with Him in relationship, and lives according to His ways. The joy that righteousness brings is ultimately in the awareness that all is well with God. There's really no greater joy than being in right standing with Him.

I've often said to my friends when I arrive at the first tee, "I come with high hopes and low expectations." It's very true for my golf game. However, when it comes to walking with God, I live with high hopes that His goodness extends to even me, and high expectations that it will always be that way.

◈

Lord, I say a heartfelt thank You for the joy that comes with belonging to You. While I long to daily please You, I sometimes fail and feel defeated. But then I remember that You said, "I will never leave you nor forsake you" (Hebrews 15:5 ESV), and the joy returns. Thank You that there's always hope in You and You alone. Amen.

39

CONQUERORS

*In all these things we are more than
conquerors through Him who loved us.*

Romans 8:37 NKJV

At the end of a televised pro-golf tournament, the winner tipped his hat and waved to the massive, cheering gallery that lined the fairway as he walked to the final green. His score was an astounding 27 under par with 6 shots separating him from the rest of the field. During the walk up, the broadcast host offered some deserved flowery words about the victor that included a phrase that sounded familiar. He said, "What we have watched is a player who has more than conquered the course over the last four days—he has absolutely owned it!"

The three-word expression that caught my ear

was *more than conquered*. It's a phrase used by the apostle Paul in reference to those who have put their faith and trust in Jesus. But what does it mean to be "more than conquerors"? The answer is in the verses that precede and follow Romans 8:37.

> If God is for us, who can be against us? He who did not spare His own Son, but delivered Him up for us all, how shall He not with Him also freely give us all things? Who shall bring a charge against God's elect? It is God who justifies. Who is he who condemns? It is Christ who died, and furthermore is also risen, who is even at the right hand of God, who also makes intercession for us. Who shall separate us from the love of Christ? Shall tribulation, or distress, or persecution, or famine, or nakedness, or peril, or sword?...For I am persuaded that neither death nor life, nor angels nor principalities nor powers, nor things present nor things to come, nor height nor depth, nor any other created thing, shall be able to separate us from the love of God which is in Christ Jesus our Lord (verses 31-35, 38-39 NKJV).

Paul wanted the believers to understand that belonging to Christ meant having some huge advantages when it came to overcoming the troubles they were facing. And considering the God-granted advantages that he listed, it's no wonder that he would refer to Christians as "more than conquerors." The good news is, it's a title that still applies to everyone who puts their faith and trust in Jesus.

◈

Father in heaven, I offer my deepest thanks that because of Your precious and mighty Son, Jesus, who conquered death and the grave, I am not only Your child but I have been made more than a conqueror through Him. I admit that without Christ it would not be so, and I confess I need His presence in my life to continue being victorious over the tribulation that this world can often bring. In His name I pray. Amen.

40

THE PRE-SHOT ROUTINE

*When Daniel knew that the document had
been signed, he went to his house where he
had windows in his upper chamber open
toward Jerusalem. He got down on his knees
three times a day and prayed and gave thanks
before his God, as he had done previously.*

DANIEL 6:10 ESV

There is a phrase in today's passage that golfers
can relate to. In reference to Daniel's daily regimen of prayer and thanksgiving, the closing line of
text says: "as he had done previously." In other words,
the great prophet had a routine that he followed.

Golfers can appreciate Daniel's consistent
approach to communicating with God because
we recognize the value of a routine, especially during play. It's certainly noticeable at the professional

level, and it's undeniable that following a routine has helped many pro golfers be consistent and excel at the game.

Consider, for example, the foot-to-foot rocking that Patrick Cantlay does just before he putts. Or there's the "sneak up" to the ball that Billy Horshel chooses to do as he prepares to putt. Then there's the one-quarter backswing and check of his club head position that Justin Thomas repeats before he hits his driver and irons. For each of these players, there's something about being diligent to do what they've "done previously" that greatly benefits their stroke. It's called refocusing.

In the case of Daniel, with so much going on in his life that challenged his commitment to God, he had plenty of reasons to regularly be on his knees in prayer and thanksgiving. From being exiled from Jerusalem when King Nebuchadnezzar besieged the city, to facing the threat of death by lions for not bowing to a man-made statue, to the stress of being called on to successfully and accurately interpret the king's visions and dreams, Daniel's attention was consumed.

Determined to not be guilty of forsaking his

God amid all the stress, Daniel went often to his altar. And it's important to note that he didn't start the three-times-a-day regimen when the hard times came. Instead, to keep his head "in the game," he had been doing it all along and he stuck with it, sort of like Cantlay, Horshel, Thomas, and any other golfer does in order to refocus.

The question Daniel's example brings up is, can it be said of you and me that "he got down on his knees three times a day and prayed and gave thanks before his God, as he had done previously"? If not, now is the time to begin. It may not involve going to our physical knees to pray and give thanks, but our spiritual knees are just as usable. And as golfers, what better reminder to engage with God regularly than our own personal pre-shot routine?

❖

Father in heaven, as Psalm 100 urges me to do, I need to often enter Your gates with thanksgiving and Your courts with praise; to give thanks You and praise Your name. In these chaotic times filled with political and social madness, along with the everyday responsibilities that consume my attention, I know I need to daily refocus on You, O Lord. May it be so in the name of Your Son, Jesus. Amen.

41

WHAT A HUG!

The joy of the LORD is your strength.

NEHEMIAH 8:10 NIV

Nehemiah's statement in today's verse was made to those who had gathered at the celebration of the newly rebuilt temple in Jerusalem. Instead of being jubilant, however, the people were weeping because they had lived without the Law for such a long time while they were in exile.

Seeing they were downcast and wanting them to rejoice and thank God for His protection and provision, Nehemiah said, "Go your way, eat the fat, and drink the sweet, and send portions unto them for whom nothing is prepared: for this day is holy unto our LORD: neither be ye sorry; for the joy of the LORD is your strength" (KJV).

The last phrase of the verse can be encouraging

in more ways than one. The original purpose for the powerful words was to remind the people that having the Lord and His great goodness as their sole reason for cheer was their ultimate source of strength both bodily and spiritually. It's still true today. His kindness alone is enough to motivate us to not be weary, to walk and not faint.

As mentioned, there is another way that Nehemiah's words can be viewed. As a disclaimer, this interpretation departs from the actual meaning, but it offers an intriguing and hopefully encouraging thought especially when applied to our relationship to God as His children. And the best way to explain it is to refer to the legendary Tiger Woods and his dad, Earl Woods.

In 1997, Tiger won his first Masters tournament. As he walked off the eighteenth green, he found his dad and they embraced. Their tight, lingering, tearful hug moved everyone who saw it. In those unforgettable moments, it wasn't easy to tell who was happiest—the young Tiger or the elder Mr. Woods. What does this have to do with Nehemiah's well-known words?

Consider this. Earl Woods had invested untold

hours, years, and resources into his son's golf game. Then, when crunch time came and his son drew on all that his dad had poured into him, and he battled through to the end of the world's most prestigious competition in golf as the victor, someone could have said to Tiger, "The joy of your dad is in the incredible strength that you displayed today."

Any parent who has helped a child learn a skill and then watched in amazement as they showed poise and power while using it can relate to how Earl Woods felt that day in Augusta. With that imagery in mind, perhaps you can see how the joy of our Lord could be found in His children's confident use of His strength that He poured into us to help us be victorious over the things of this world that challenge our faith. And what a hug is in store for us when we finish our "final round."

❖

Father in heaven, nothing would please me more than to be pleasing to You. I offer my deepest thanks for all You've taught me through Your written Word about how to live this life righteously. I want to use that insight as a source of strength and enlist it in times when my faith is tested. I truly want my usage of Your strength to bring You joy. May it be so in the name of Jesus. Amen.

42

THE CADDIE

*The Helper, the Holy Spirit, whom the
Father will send in My name, He will
teach you all things, and bring to your
remembrance all things that I said to you.*

JOHN 14:26 NKJV

I am among the throngs of golf enthusiasts who
have never had the privilege of playing a round
with the aid of a caddie. Only in my imagination
have I left the first tee box after a drive with a caddie
at my side, taking my club and wiping it clean as he
slips it back into my bag, all the while feeling the
strap cutting into his shoulder, not mine, as I stroll
unencumbered down the fairway, free to think only
about shot number two. How sweet is that fantasy.
All I can say is, "Dream on!"

Whenever I watch a tournament on TV, it's

enjoyable to observe the teamwork between the player and his skilled assistant. And it's especially interesting when high-quality microphones that are nearby pick up the conversations between the pair.

Their overheard exchanges make it clear that the job of the caddie goes well beyond helping his contender conserve energy by toting his heavy, colorful, personalized, brand-marked bag. They bring experience and knowledge of the course to pass along, records of pre-tournament calculations of approach shot distances, and reminders of putting surface slopes and speed. They even help control the distracting noise of the gallery.

Besides being a wealth of knowledge for the player, a good caddie will carefully observe the demeanor of his "boss" to help with offering encouraging words when the round has gone sour. These, and all the other responsibilities a caddie has, are all covered for one purpose—to help the player win by saving strokes.

With a caddie's main function being a helper, how appropriate it is to compare their role to that of the Holy Spirit, whom, Jesus said, "The Father will send in My name, He will teach you all things, and bring to your remembrance all things I said to you."

What an incredibly kind thing for God to do for His followers. He did it because He knows very well that we can't play the round of life successfully without the Helper. Thankfully, enlisting the aid of the "divine Caddie" is not a dream we can only wish would come true. His assistance is promised, and with Him winning is guaranteed. "Let it be so!"

◈

Father in heaven, thank You for sending me the Helper, Your Holy Spirit, who will—with endless wisdom and unfailing strength—help me walk so as to be pleasing to You. I want to listen to His voice of instruction and follow His guidance throughout my life. May it be so to Your glory in the name of Your beloved Son. Amen.

43

REGRETS

Godly sorrow brings repentance that leads
to salvation and leaves no regret.

2 Corinthians 7:10 niv

More than once I've left a course after 18 holes of golf and, as I replay the entire round in my head shot by shot, I'm haunted by regret over a particular decision I made during play. As an example, I was in a foursome at a familiar course, and on hole number six I hit my drive to the right side of the fairway among some trees.

Par was 4 for the hole, and when I got to my ball I could see the green through an opening between two huge oak trees—but there were low-hanging branches that prevented any type of lofted shot. I realized for shot number two I could put the ball in the back of my stance and hit a low flyer and, if I was fortunate, my ball would roll up and onto the elevated putting surface.

In an effort to cover the 120 yards to the green, I knew I had to hit it hard and firm. Unfortunately, I got more turf behind the ball than I intended, and my club blade opened just enough to send my low-launched ball toward the oak on the right. The ball ricocheted sharply and much to my displeasure it ended up on the adjacent fairway. If I could have, I would have blamed anyone but me for the disappointing double, but it was my bad and I had to own it.

As I mentally replayed hole six and that second embarrassing shot, I remembered something that made me a little mad at myself. I recalled looking to the left of the two big oaks and seeing that there was a clear shot back into the fairway that angled toward the green. This option would have made my third shot a doable 90 yards. I would have had a much better chance of dropping a wedge in close to the hole from that distance. But no...I had to try the hero shot between the trees.

If you play golf regularly, there is no doubt that after reading about my fiasco on number six you're thinking, *Been there, regretted that!* We all have felt that grinding in the gut when we realize we knew we had a better shot choice but didn't take it. That type of regret might be the worst kind in golf, but regret hurts far worse when it involves a wrong decision made off the golf course.

Undoubtedly, we have all made choices we regret. From actions taken that led to trouble, to hurtful words said to someone, to major purchases that weren't wise, we have "shots" we wish we could redo. They're a part of life. Thankfully, however, when it comes to faith and spiritual matters, there is a decision that many of us have made for which we never, ever should feel sorry. It was revealed in Paul's divinely led teaching to the Corinthians when he said, "Godly sorrow brings repentance that leads to salvation and leaves no regret."

Godly sorrow is the work of the Holy Spirit guiding us to a realization that something's not right in our hearts, and when we seek God's for-giveness as a response to that awareness, we are led to the joy of salvation. There's never a need to sec-ond-guess whether it was the right thing to do. And best of all, the reward for making such a wise and eternally rewarding "shot choice" is that we'll never, ever regret it.

O Father in heaven, how thankful I am for the day I sensed the kind of sorrow You regard as right and that it led me to a desire to ask You for forgiveness of my sins. Not for one instant do I regret making that choice. I bless You for loving me enough to hear my prayer of repentance, and I pray that as I journey onward You will help me remain faithful to You. Amen.

44

SHORT OF THE GREEN

All have sinned, and come short of the glory of God.

ROMANS 3:23 KJV

There are at least two phrases in Romans 3:23 that every avid golfer can appreciate. First, as I mentioned in chapter 12, the words "all have sinned" have their roots in an archery term that means "to miss the mark." Most golfers would likely agree that, had the game been in existence when Paul was looking for an illustration of sin, he could have chosen the picture of an approach shot from the fairway to the green that was intended to drop within a foot of the pin or, better yet, be slam-dunked into the hole, but, instead, it lands way short of the putting surface or painfully 60 feet right or left of the flag.

Without exception, "all have hit a wayward

shot" like this, which leads to the second phrase in the verse that golfers easily grasp—the words "and come short of the glory of God."

Because golf is a game that requires precise measurements, yards, feet, and inches are constantly in our mental calculators. These distances are programmed into our handheld range finders and are written in the books tournament players carry in their back pockets. The numbers are there for one purpose—to assist the shooter in not coming short of an intended target. Yet, all—including both pros and amateurs—have failed to hit the mark more times than any care to admit.

On the surface, hearing that "all have sinned and come short of the glory of God" sounds negative and could be considered as a reason to lose hope. However, in reality, it's a verse filled with great hope—and here's why. It instructs each and every one of us that humanity is prone to sin and does not measure up to the standard of God as defined by His Word. And, because we all fall short of the glory of God, we need a way that we can measure up to it.

Enter Jesus, who came to earth to live a faultless life that perfectly reflected God's glory. And that's just what He did. Then, as proof of His great love for all whose best "shots" at being righteous fail to land anywhere near that green, He did something amazing. He bore our sins in His body on the cross so that we, in Him, might die to sin and live to righteousness. It's because of Christ, and Him alone, that we can now measure up to the character (glory) of God.

Blessed be the name of the Lord for His great grace and mercy that never fall short of our desperate need for forgiveness.

Thank You, Jesus, for understanding that I have failed to reach the righteousness You long for me to display. You are indeed a kind and compassionate Savior who has graciously given me the blessing of Your redeeming grace. It's because of You, and You alone, that I can reach Your standard of holiness. Thank You for hitting that mark for me. Amen.

45

THE UNFAIR-WAY

These things I have spoken to you so that in Me you may have peace. In the world you have tribulation, but take courage; I have overcome the world.

JOHN 16:33

A wise golf instructor would do every new player a great favor by giving them a heads up that there's trouble and sorrow waiting for them on the course. The student needs to know that at times the tee box will be the "calami-tee box" and the fairway will sometimes feel more like the "unfair-way."

Making a newbie aware in advance that their "blowup hole" is waiting to be reached is important. But before they encounter the frustrations and disappointments that come with inevitable golf woes, they should be given some hope to lean on in order to find peace when, for example, a drive finds the deep rough or a bladed greenside chip darts like a bullet by the hole. Where is that hope? It's found in what the teacher tells their student in advance of the adversity.

If the student has been assured all along that no matter what trouble he finds on the golf course his teacher will not hate or abandon him, then he can relax and enjoy learning and playing the game. The confidence this promise fosters in the student is a great picture of the assurance that the disciples of Christ were given when they heard Him say, "These things I have spoken to you so that in Me you may have peace." The question is, what things had He spoken?

The entire chapter of John 16 is a record of Jesus assuring His disciples that even though He would soon be returning to the One who had sent Him, and though they would no longer see Him with eyes of flesh, He would send His Holy Spirit to them who would guide them into all truth (verse 13). Best of all, they would not be left alone.

To further comfort them in the grief they felt over their Master's impending physical absence, Jesus said, "The Father Himself loves you, because you have loved Me and have believed that I came forth from the Father" (John 16:27). In other words, no matter what happened, no matter how bad things got, God's love for them would never wane.

Playing golf is a worthy way to often be reminded that "in this world you will have trouble" (NIV). The game is full of it. But it's also a game that can help us remember that as bad as things might get on the course of this life, we are no less loved by our Divine Teacher who has promised that we are not alone when the fairway becomes the "unfair-way."

❖

Thank You, Father, for the promise of Your never-ending, never-failing love that can keep my heart at peace even in the face of tribulation. I will gratefully lean on Your love and trust that it will be with me all the days of my life…especially in the hard times. What a comfort it is to know that when trouble comes, You have already overcome it. Blessed be Your name. Amen.

46

THE SIN TRAP

By his wicked plan an evil man is trapped,
but the righteous man sings and rejoices
[for his plan brings good things to him].

PROVERBS 29:6 AMP

Some shots in the game of golf are dreaded by most players. Trying to not thin a tight lie, powering through a deep rough, attempting a long iron shot through a narrow space between trees, digging out of a divot, or flying the ball over water are all situations that can mess with the mind and ultimately the swing. But there's one shot, especially for the casual golfer, that seems to bring on anxiety more than all the others. It's the one out of the feared sand trap.

Usually, the dread of hitting "off the beach" is a product of not really knowing how to execute the shot, and the end result of that lack of skill can be just that—an ugly execution that kills the score. As unwanted as a sand-trapped shot is to most of us who golf, there's something redeemable to learn from it in light of Proverbs 29:6.

The first half of the verse says, "By his wicked plan an evil man is *trapped*" (emphasis added). The difference between the trap that a golfer and an evil man gets in is obvious. A golfer doesn't plan an errant shot. An evil man, on the other hand, devises wickedness and traps himself in it.

It seems that if a person clearly understood that planning to do wrong will land them in a "sin trap," wouldn't it be smart to avoid such a consequence? Yet even at this moment people are deliberately making ungodly choices that have "spiritual blowup hole" written all over them. May it not be so for you or me.

The second half of the verse offers wisdom to all who will take heed. It says, "But the righteous man sings and rejoices [for his plan brings good things to him]." To put it in golf terms, we all know that a well-strategized, well-hit lob over a greenside bunker can bring a song of joy to a player, especially when it rolls up to the hole, as planned, within tap-in distance.

In a similar way, so can a person's heart sing the song of gladness when they wisely and successfully plan to avoid the self-destructive trap of transgression. The "good things" that come as a result include knowing that their plan was pleasing to the Lord and that their actions testify to others of the grace of God. May it be so for you and me.

◈

Thank You, God, for the wisdom and the warning given in the words of this proverb. You know that the desire of my heart is to always avoid landing myself in a sin trap. I need Your grace and guidance to help me do it, but I also need Your mercy and forgiveness when I fail. In the name of Your precious Son, Jesus, I pray. Amen.

47

A MAN AND HIS PLANS

Many are the plans in the mind of a man,
but it is the purpose of the LORD that will stand.

PROVERBS 19:21 ESV

As I drove our cart away from the thirteenth green and headed to the fourteenth tee, my friend Don was tallying up the score on his card. When he finished, he tossed it into the cart's cubbyhole in a way that told me he wasn't pleased with the number at that point. When I stopped and set the parking brake, he said something that sounded all too familiar.

"Last night and this morning before I got here, I mentally played every hole in preparation for this round. I know these fairways well enough to know where the best places are to put the ball, and I've putted on these greens enough times to read them right—but what good did it do? The total on my card to this point is nowhere close to what I wanted it to be."

It was as though my friend were using his mouth to say what I was thinking. I, too, had formed my game plan before arriving at the course only to face the disappointing reality that I'd be leaving with unfulfilled expectations.

I wondered how many others in our group of 12 players that day had arrived at the first tee with their carefully thought through, pre-round prep. And I wondered how many were finishing up with the thought, *Well, it's back to the drawing board.*

When I thought later about our round of golf and the less-than-stellar outcomes my friend and I dealt with, I realized we had lived an illustration of Proverbs 19:21 that says, "Many are the plans in the mind of a man, but it is the purpose of the LORD that will stand."

Notice that the verse doesn't say, "Man shouldn't make his plans." Instead, it says, "Many are the plans in the mind of a man." God permits us to think ahead—even about how to play a round of golf. We're not to feel condemned for mentally plotting our steps. Not only is it good, but it's also wise to do. The question is, do we know who is ultimately in charge of our lives—and why?

In golf, it could be said that the course determines the path we follow, but when it comes to the course of our days, it's God who has the ultimate say about how we, as His children, fit into His purpose. For that reason, He can alter our way if He so desires. But because we can completely trust that His plan for each of us is to our benefit, and that only His purpose will stand the test of time, it's to our great advantage to let Him prevail over our walk on the fairway of life.

In the New Testament, James alluded to the truth contained in Proverbs 19:21 when he wrote,

> Listen, you who say, "Today or tomorrow we will go to this or that city, spend a year there, carry on business and make money." Why, you do not even know what will happen tomorrow. What is your life? You are a mist that appears for a little while and then vanishes. Instead, you ought to say, "If it is the Lord's will, we will live and do this or that" (James 4:13-15 NIV).

The wisdom of James should behoove us to remember that, as we make plans for various reasons and motives, we can't predict the outcome. That reality can make us worry and fret about the future if we let it. The best way to not grind over it is to tag all of our stated plans with a two-word statement that reveals an awareness of, and submission to, God's good and lasting plan for us. Those two words are often heard in our group after a round is completed and we're looking ahead to the next outing. "Enjoyed it. See you next time, *Lord willing*."

◈

God, You know that I make plans, and even though they might be good, I want to hold them with an open hand. I want to always be willing to submit my plans to You and trust that if You have another course for me to walk, it will be for my good. I desire this because I know that Your plans will not fail. May it be so in Your loving name. Amen!

48

DRESSED RIGHT

*I will rejoice greatly in the LORD, my soul
will be joyful in my God; for He has clothed
me with garments of salvation, He has
wrapped me with a robe of righteousness.*

ISAIAH 61:10

It's widely understood that attending the Masters tournament in Augusta, Georgia, requires the patron (not *fan*) to follow a certain dress code. The general rule is "dress as though you're playing." That means arriving and walking the grounds in attire that includes collared shirts and long pants or shorts that are considered golf shorts. Jeans are not acceptable, and any hat worn must not be turned backwards.

This long-held and strongly enforced dress code has not only served to strengthen the status of the

Masters as the globe's most prestigious golf tournament, but it has also influenced the entire world of golfing in terms of fashion. Perhaps one of the reasons this is true is because the paradise-like environment of Augusta and many other courses deserves the respect of its players and visitors when it comes to their appearance.

Because of this tradition of reflecting a reverence for well-maintained property, most golfers willingly comply with not showing up shabby to the courses they frequent. And most would agree that keeping that tradition can even help create a more focused mindset that leads to better play.

Speaking of not showing up shabby at the Masters and courses like it, there's another paradise that has a dress code for entering, and it is even more stringent. That place is called *heaven*. Commonly and biblically known as the place where God dwells, there will be no toleration for spiritual shabbiness there. To put it another way, unrighteousness will not be permitted on heaven's "grounds."

In reference to the city of God, Revelation 21:27 says, "Nothing unclean, and no one who practices abomination and lying, shall ever come into it, but only those whose names are written in the Lamb's book of life." That announcement can be disconcerting for all of us, to say the least, because we all sin and come short of God's character (Romans 3:23). Where do we go to get the spiritual attire needed for entering heaven? There's good news to give as the answer.

Isaiah 61:10 reveals that we can rejoice in the fact that because of God's provision of His Son, Jesus, and the completed work of atonement for sin via the cross, burial, and resurrection, we who have accepted that atonement have been given the clothing necessary for entrance into heaven. It's called "a robe of righteousness."

It's not our garment of righteousness that satisfies God's dress code because "all of us have become like one who is unclean, and all our righteous acts are like filthy rags" (Isaiah 64:6 NIV). Instead, the clothing we will wear to enter the gates of heaven is the robe of the righteousness of Jesus that is wrapped around us when we repent of sin and receive His forgiveness. What good news indeed!

When we get dressed in our best to head to the gates of our favorite course, let it remind us that we who are redeemed are dressed already for the paradise that awaits us beyond this life. It's a place that has no real rival when it comes to beauty and sacredness, including Augusta.

❖

Thanks be to You, almighty and compassionate God, for providing the attire of Your Son's righteousness that is required to enter the place where You dwell. I wear that robe with gratitude and will remain humbled by such a gracious gift. Blessed be Your name. Amen.

49

FIRST TEE

*Be anxious for nothing, but in everything by prayer
and supplication, with thanksgiving, let your
requests be made known to God; and the peace
of God, which surpasses all understanding, will
guard your hearts and minds through Christ Jesus.*

PHILIPPIANS 4:6-7 NKJV

As an avid golfer, when I read the first four words of Philippians 4:6 that instructs, "Be anxious for nothing," something in me whispers, *Yeah, right. If the apostle Paul would've experienced first tee jitters, would he have said such a thing?*

Of course, I ask that question tongue in cheek but, honestly, how I wish I could bring into play (pun intended) those four words on number one when the gallery of guys I'm golfing with is watching. The craving to hit one straight and as long as possible can be intensely unsettling as I silently, quickly, and nervously go down the swing technique checklist.

- Target chosen? Check.

- Set up good? Check.

- Feet are wide enough? Check.

- Strong grip? Check.

- Ball placement on the left heel? Check.

- Don't forget a long and low-to-the-ground takeaway. Check.

- Hip rotation timing has to be perfect. Check.

- Follow through. Please!

All those mental meanderings lead to one final thought just before the swing is made: *Don't be the one to prove that the word* golf *is an acrostic for, "Go Out, Look Foolish."*

I can't remember not being anxious on the first tee, and I don't think I will ever be at total peace on that challenging spot. But that's golf. It's hard to play well, and the truth is, why would I play if it didn't test the steel in my nerves? But life is hard too. It has its reasons for a "player" to be anxious. From matters concerning health of the body, to the health of the family, to the security of a vocation, most of us live on the first tee.

Thankfully, though, Paul wasn't talking about golf with his "be anxious for nothing" admonishment. He was referring to God's ability and willingness to provide His people with whatever is needed to live daily—and our resting in that promise yields a kind of peace that can't be fully understood or explained.

When His provision is sought through prayers of thanksgiving and bold asking, that inexplicable peace that comes will settle the most anxious of minds. It's a truth and a promise that can be remembered and celebrated each time a golfer hears, "You're up!"

◈

What cause for joy I have, Lord, that You want to provide my every need in life. So, with a thankful heart I make my requests known to You, and I bless You for the peace it brings, and that it's an assurance that will guard my heart and mind and keep worry at bay. To You be all the glory for such marvelous love toward me! Amen.

50

FINISH WELL

His lord said unto him, Well done, thou good
and faithful servant: thou hast been faithful
over a few things, I will make thee ruler over
many things: enter thou into the joy of thy lord.

MATTHEW 25:21 KJV

Golf is a game where the winner is not the *most perfect* with their play. The one who wins the trophy is the one who is *least imperfect*. In other words, there's not a player alive today or in the past or future that can boast that all their rounds, all their shots, and all their putts were flawless.

The same is true off the golf course. No one has or will do life perfectly, especially when it comes to our spiritual journey. The fact is, when we get to heaven, not one of us will hear, "Best done thou good and faithful servant." The best we'll get is "well done." Only one has done life best. His name is Jesus.

Though none can boast of perfection in golf, that fact doesn't deter any of us from making our best effort to strive to do better. We all want to finish each round as well as we can and, in order to do so, we actively work at eliminating bad swing habits and hindering thoughts that cause us trouble. We do it so that when it's over we can say we did everything we could to finish well.

It should be no different in our spiritual life. And, to accomplish the goal of finishing well as a follower of Christ, sometimes we should do what Hebrews 12:1 says to do: "Let us lay aside every weight, and the sin which doth so easily beset us, and let us run with patience the race that is set before us" (KJV).

Just one good example of someone who understood this admonition is the grandfather in the following story told in this song lyric:

FINISH WELL

He'll turn eighty-one next Sunday,
I called him on the phone.

I said, "I'm coming to see you, Grandpa,
what can I bring along?
Would you like a dish for your TV,
would you like the internet?"
He said, "Thank you, boy, but this ain't the time to be
Trippin' over stuff like that...cause

I want to finish well.
I want to end this race
Still leaning on His amazing grace.
I want these last few miles to testify
that God never fails.
I don't want to fall down this close to the line.
I want to finish well.

But you can bring me a Bible
Where the words are big and tall,
So these old eyes can read the truth
That will help me not to fall.

I want to finish well.
I want to end this race
Still leaning on His amazing grace.
I want these last few miles to testify
that God never fails.
I don't want to fall down this close to the line.
I want to finish well."[4]

The grandfather knew that access to the internet could be a spiritual hindrance and could make him stumble and for those reasons he refused it. The question for the rest of us is, what bad habits, thoughts, beliefs, or actions do we need to avoid or eliminate in order to hear "well done" from God when our round of life is complete?

Likely, each one of us can immediately name the encumbrance or sin that can so easily trip us up. As we approach our final "eighteenth," may we enlist all the patience we can muster to lay it aside for the sake of winning the prize of a home in heaven.

❖

Father, I'm grateful for the hope that someday I can hear You say, "Well done." I know that it will happen only because I have put my trust in You. I pray for the courage to lay aside those things that could hinder me from doing well, and for Your help to be faithful to You until my journey is complete. In the name of Jesus, the only perfect One, I pray. Amen.

Notes and Song Lyric Credits

1. Steve Chapman and Lindsey Williams, "You Just Never Know" © 2014 by Time & Seasons Music / Really Big Bison Music.

2. Steve Chapman, "He's Watching," © 2005 Times & Seasons Music.

3. Steve Chapman, *A Look at Life from a Deer Stand* (Eugene, OR: Harvest House Publishers, 2012), 93-94.

4. Steve Chapman, "Finish Well," © 2008 Times & Seasons Music.

For a list of available music and books or
for more information about the Chapmans,
please visit their website:

www.steveandanniechapman.com

or write to:

S&A Family
PO Box 337
Pleasant View, TN 37146

Bible Versions and Copyright Notifications

About the Author

Proudly claiming West Virginia as his home state, Steve Chapman grew up as the son of a preacher. He met his wife, Annie, in junior high school in 1963. In March of 1975, they married after dating a few months and settled in Nashville, Tennessee. There they raised their son and daughter, Nathan and Heidi.

Steve is president of S&A Family, Inc., an organization formed to oversee the production of the Chapmans' recorded music. They have had "family life" as the theme of their lyrics since they began singing together in 1980. As Dove Award-winning artists, they have traveled nationally and internationally offering concerts that feature songs from more than 20 recorded projects.

Steve is a huge fan of the outdoors with a particular interest in hunting and fishing. He is also an avid golfer and a member of the faith-based community of golfers in Nashville known as GOF (Golf Outing Fellowship). As a service to his fellow players, Steve provides golf-themed devotional writings that are featured in *A Look at Life from the Fairway*.